A History of
the Railways
of
OXFORDSHIRE
Part 2: The South

A 28XX class no 2895 heads south from Oxford station with a train of oil tank wagons. Note south box on the left and the landmark of St Barnabas' Church in the distance.

Brian Sessions

A History of the Railways of
OXFORDSHIRE
Part 2: The South

Bill Simpson

Lamplight Publications

Lamplight Publications
Witney

260 Colwell drive, Witney, Oxon OX8 7LW

First Published 2001

ISBN 1 899246 06 1

Printed at the Alden Press, Oxford

Preface

If you were to take the possible journey by railway around the county of Oxfordshire some seventy years or so ago starting at Didcot, pausing at Radley to go up the Abingdon branch, then passing up the county through Oxford to Banbury. From there along the branch to Cheltenham as far as Kingham, through Chipping Norton, back to Oxford. Then south turning at Kennington onto the Thame line leaving the county at Princes Risborough. Then to retrace on a journey to Watlington where, regrettably for the hopes and failed aspirations of the Watlington and Wallingford Railway you would have to go by road to reach Wallingford station. From Wallingford back to the main line and take a trip up the branch to Henley. What would have been revealed to the privileged vista of the rail traveller would be the diversity of the landscape of the county, the rugged redlands to the north joining the county to Northamptonshire. Compared with the gentler slopes of the south leading to Berkshire, apart from the brighter stone slopes of Shotover. In other words the county would provide variety in landscape. This volume together with the earlier volume 1 of the North will, I hope, reveal the pleasure of that variety, so marked between college Oxford and William Morris car works at Oxford. How gratifying and enriching would such an easy paced journey be if it could be undertaken today. I hope these volumes will inspire the imagination to experience it in these pages.

Bill Simpson
Bicester 2001

Acknowledgements

The Author would like to convey his thanks to the following for their generous support in compiling this volume; Ken Bampton, Les Burley, H C Casserley, R M Casserley, F G Cockman, Bruce Coleman, Geoff Gamble, Oxfordshire County Council Photographic Archive, Frank Jones, Laurence Waters, Des Perry, Bill Peto (GWS), Dick Riley and owners of photographic collections for kindly allowing prints of theirs to be used.
Prints from Mowat Collection available from Brunel University Transport Collection W R Burton, 3 fairway, Clifton, York, YO30 5QA

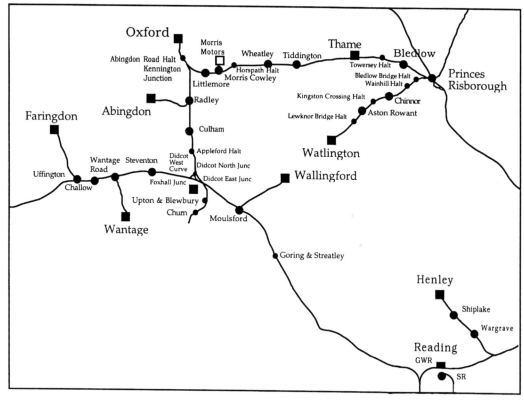

Layout of the lines in Oxfordshire covered by this book.

CONTENTS

A Dukedog no 9015 passes through Oxford station on a freight train on February 27, 1954

R J Buckley

CHAPTER ONE

OXFORD

A branch to Oxford of twelve miles was included in the Prospectus of the Great Western Railway in 1833, to build a railway from London to Bristol, so it was clear from the outset that the Company was seeking to include the capital of academia within its territory. The GWR was finally incorporated as a Company in 1835. The competing port of Liverpool had received railway connection with Manchester in 1829 so it was imperative that Bristol had its connection also to London.

After the Bill for the building of the railway from London to Bristol received the Royal Assent on August 31, 1835 little time was wasted in getting the works going. The GWR were well aware that the London & Birmingham Railway, under the young but powerful influence of Robert Stephenson, was proceeding on its course from London in June 1834 and by 1835 was well under construction. This was built in the Stephenson chosen gauge of 4ft 8½in. Whereas Isambard Kingdom Brunel, Chief Engineer of the GWR, was building his line in the gauge of

7ft ¼in gauge. This would be a source of conflict between the railways although the men themselves were good friends.

In 1837 a Bill for an Oxford Railway went before parliament, the route chosen was from Didcot alongside the Thames through the village of Iffley and by the Cowley Road to a station close to Magdalen Bridge at The Plain. This was flying in the face of a very strong opposition to the railway in principle by prominent academics who reacted most vociferously and forestalled this scheme. Further opposition was added later from the House of Lords, by the Duke of Wellington, Chancellor of the University.

This plan included a branch to Abingdon. Brunel was forced to modify this route and in another scheme chose land east of the Abingdon Road near Folly Bridge in 1839. This revision to some degree pacified the university but inflamed two landowners in the House of Lords Captain Pechell and Sir G Bowyer, who owned 4½ miles of the 9½ mile route giving them collective strength to cause a revision of that plan.

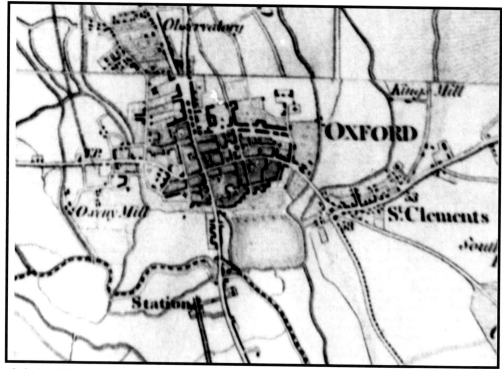

Oxford in 1846, the station is well south of the River Thames. The first survey favoured by Brunel was where the roads join in St Clements. The eventual route of the line north was just to the left of the line coming south to the Botley Road, this is the proposed route of the Buckinghamshire Railway, the GWR went just to the left of this with their 1852 station.

Another plan of 1840 shows the same route with two approaches to the Abingdon branch, one from the Oxford direction and another from the Didcot direction. The Abingdon branch was receiving no better welcome than a railway at Oxford, being opposed by towns-people led by Mr Duffield, MP for Abingdon. This resulted in the branch scheme being abandoned altogether.

Whatever, the skirmishes apart, the GWR opened their first section of the main line route between London and Maidenhead on June 4, 1838 and from there to Didcot on June 1, 1840. They had to keep in mind that the London & Birmingham line had been completed and opened in September of 1838. The GWR's complete route to Bristol was finally opened on June 30, 1841.

This now left Oxford with its rail access being ten miles away at Steventon to which horse drawn coaches shuttled back and forth to make connection with the trains carrying many university students beyond the confines of the University.

Once again, after proving the permanence and effectiveness of the new railway the GWR promoted a branch to Oxford in 1842, the Oxford Railway. This time with a station in fields to the west of the Abingdon Road in an area known as Grandpont. Some opposition polarised this time in the form of the Warden of Wadham College as Chairman of the Oxford Canal Committee, otherwise the University was largely in favour with provisional clauses such as the following:

'For the preservation of University discipline that the Vice-Chancellor, Proctors or Proproctors, Heads of Colleges and Halls or their deputies and the Marshal of the University should have free access to all stations at train times to ascertain if any members of the University were travelling or attempting to do so, and forbade the Company to convey any such members below the degrees of Master of Arts or Bachelor of Civil Law as should be pointed out by such officers for a period of twenty-four hours, even if their fares have been paid, or to take up or set down any members below these degrees except at the regular stations, under a penalty of £5 for each offence.'

Power to lease or sell the line to the GWR

were stipulated, and an early amalgamation was intended. The entire capital was put up by the Great Western in the names of ten of their Directors there being no local shareholders. The Oxford Railway Company was dissolved by Royal Assent on May 10, 1844.

Assents were obtained from the landowners concerned, the only petitions lodged in opposition were from the Corporation of Oxford and some 300 inhabitants of the city which was organised by the Oxford Canal Company. To counteract this a petition was organised in favour which bore the signatures of some 1,500 inhabitants.

The Bill received the Royal Assent on April 11, 1843. Work commenced in October and proceeded rapidly throughout the mild winter. The only engineering works of any importance were the bridges over the Thames at Appleford and Nuneham, both were constructed entirely of timber.

The entire branch of some 9 miles 57 chains in length was completed in June and was inspected on the 10th by Major-General Pasley accompanied by Brunel and several Directors. The only fault noted by the Inspector was the insecure state of a bridge carrying the Oxford - Abingdon turnpike road above the line. This concerns the manipulations of an individual constructing a paper house on the line of the embankment to carry the road above the railway in order to secure compensation from the company. The completion of the bridge was delayed whilst the individual was legally dismissed. The line was officially opened June 12, 1844 with a grand banquet at the Angel Hotel, Oxford. Immediately thirty horse omnibuses began running from the station over a wide area including Cheltenham and Leamington, one as far as Rugby!

On the same day a large junction station was opened at Didcot consisting of four lines and five very narrow platforms under an all-over roof.

Intermediate stations were opened at Appleford, two miles from Didcot, immediately south of the first over-bridge on the branch. The next was Abingdon Road, three miles from Didcot. The first station at Appleford was closed in February 1849. Abingdon Road later was renamed Culham

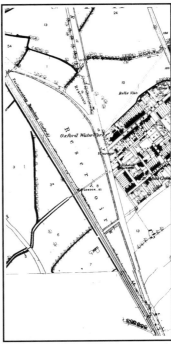

Millstream Junction where the lines joined. The original station site is the branch on the right, by this time in 1870 the area was defunct and eventually sold off, now occupied by houses, but Marlborough Road runs parallel to the trackbed.

Reproduced by kind permission of Ordnance Survey, Crown Copyright NC/01/479

on the opening of the Abingdon branch on June 2, 1856. A new Appleford station was opened on September 11, 1933, it was renamed Appleford Halt on May 5, 1964.

The Oxford terminus was a wooden structure with a large goods shed beyond it, the line was continued almost to the bank of the River Thames. This station ceased to be used for passengers when the new station, north of the river, opened in 1852. It remained as Oxford Goods station for a further twenty years until it was closed and the land was sold off.

As the Oxford branch was being built the GWR were contemplating its extension north of the River Thames or Isis by promoting two companies to extend into territories that if ignored would certainly be entered by the 'narrow' gauge London & Birmingham Railway. At the outset GWR had promulgated their lines extending to Gloucester, Cheltenham, Stroud and Trowbridge. By choosing a different gauge from the other railways it put them on the defensive by this as well as territory. If ever a standard gauge were to be adopted then the greater mileage would be bound to win the day. In fact this is exactly what did happen and it was the promotions north of Oxford that brought it to a head. The two schemes were the Oxford & Rugby and the Oxford, Worcester & Wolverhampton Railways. The Bills for these companies were laid before parliament in 1845. The L&B immediately reacted to this 'broad gauge' incursion by promoting a London Worcester and South Staffordshire Railway with a branch from Bicester to Oxford and to Rugby, further in a state of pique suggesting continuing the Bicester branch further south to Didcot and eventually connecting with the narrow gauge Basingstoke and Southampton Railway. This clash became notorious as the 'Gauge War' and saw the GWR in a speculative alliance with the Grand Junction Railway in the north in prospect of carrying the broad gauge railway far into territories it had not, at the outset, dreamt of going to. This, as it transpired, was merely a ploy by Captain Mark Huish of the Grand Junction Railway who was wishing to force the competitive line of the London & Birmingham Railway in a lucrative alliance with his own. In this he was successful and, after supporting the two schemes of the GWR, he then opposed them as Secretary of the newly formed London & North Western Railway.

The conclusion of the alliance was that the GWR did not go to Rugby but to Birmingham instead, and to Worcester and Wolverhampton, but the pure broad gauge got no further than Banbury where the Oxford & Rugby opened a station on September 2, 1850 on a single set of rails from Oxford. The Oxford & Birmingham Railway which Huish had at first supported did not melt away with his betrayal but encouraged the alliance with the GWR to go to Birmingham and joined with them at Fenny Compton, about eight miles north of Banbury, but in mixed gauge. As a result of the conflict the London & Birmingham had not been able to expand beyond Banbury, but were able to force a clause on the broad gauge for the insertion of a third rail inside to produce the capability of running the Stephenson gauge trains. This was between Banbury and Millstream Junction

south of Oxford. It was of no use to them, but forced a mortal blow on the broad gauge with this clause. And as events transpired it sowed the first seeds of its downfall.

In order to resolve the prospect of a terrible muddle the government appointed Gauge Commissioners to look into, and report on, the gauge question. This they did, but the result was conjectural. In principle opposing the broad gauge with the lesser mileage but allowing such schemes in development to continue. As a result of the Gauge Act of 1846 the GWR were forbidden to carry the broad gauge further north than Wolverhampton. However in its territorial battles the GWR acquired the Shrewsbury & Birmingham and Shrewsbury & Chester lines by an Act of 1854, both narrow gauge schemes. There from connecting these south along the Birmingham and Oxford, Oxford & Rugby to Didcot and on to Basingstoke would require the mixed gauge arrangement on that route.

Further gall was added with the other scheme of the Oxford, Worcester & Wolverhampton Railway which mutinied on its supporting parent company and built its line predominantly to run in the 'narrow' gauge. Audaciously it joined with the succeeding company to the L&B, the London & North Western Railway north of Oxford with a line to Euston opening in June 1853.

The Birmingham & Oxford opened on October 1, 1852 with two lines in mixed gauge, the second set of rails in mixed gauge were put in from Banbury to Millstream Junction, near the original Oxford station, for by now a new station was built alongside that of the LNWR at Botley Road, north of the river. In the following year the GWR placed the contentious third rail inside the original set of rails from there back to Banbury bringing complete mixed gauge on the Oxford - Birmingham route.

A serious problem to the people of Oxford has always been that the city was riven with water meadows and channels emanating from the Thames, Cherwell and Windrush Rivers with serious flooding being a problem for the city, the very name 'Oxford' is for a water crossing. The foundation of the Thames Conservancy of 1866-1976 sought to bring the situation under some control which the new railway soon discovered in 1852 when the line to Birmingham was opened in October. For by November a section of the line at Kennington, south of the station, was under water. Trains then had to be stopped and the engine run round its train and push it to the water's edge. Thenceforth horses would draw the coaches through the water until the other side was reached and another engine could be coupled, the delay would cost twelve minutes. Flooding occurred again in 1875, 1882 and 1894 which stopped traffic altogether. The railway then dug flood channels beneath the line and raised it as much as could be allowed under the Abingdon Road bridge.

Up to 1840 the Thames had been navigable to Abingdon and Oxford and prosperously associated with the link of the Oxford Canal (1790) but the former fell into disuse with the competing arrival of the railway

On April 27, 1865 the Great Western Railway approached the Mayor and City Council with a view to building its Carriage and Wagon Works at Oxford. The council offered 22 acres of land at Criply Meadow alongside the railway north of the station on the west side, near Walton Well Road.

The GWR were planning to expand the track area between Paddington and Hammersmith and the existing works there would have to be demolished for this. Also the carriage and Wagon Repair Shops at Worcester had been burnt down. They were therefore looking at site options to build a central works at Reading, Didcot, Abingdon, Oxford, Swindon, Banbury and Warwick to have building and repair on one site. Oxford City Council could see that this would be of great benefit to the employment in the town. The GWR favoured Oxford at the centre of its mixture of gauge.

The plans are first mentioned in the *Oxford Times* on Saturday 10, June 1865 announcing a public meeting in the Town Hall yard which was capable of holding 5,000 people; in the event it was filled. The strength of feeling amongst the townspeople cannot be exaggerated, for the GWR were promising to bring employment for 1,300 people and to build 500 houses. True to say some of these positions would be filled by existing employ-

ees but with expansion of the works there would also be employment for locals and the spending power of such a large influx of economic force would have a dramatic effect. The population of Oxford at that time was 30,000. The meeting closed with all being in favour to a man. As a result the University opposed the plans. It is obvious that that wage rates of the locality would be seriously affected and the University, in all its various forms, was the largest single employer in the area. Much employment had been lost to Oxford with the end of the coaching and river trades due to the arrival of the railway.

The University prevailed upon the directors of the railway, especially the Chairman Richard Potter who was very much in favour of the plans, to reconsider. The townspeople realising this were incensed at the University's influence against what would be of benefit to themselves.

The University, led by professor Goldwin Smith, painted a lurid picture of the glittering pinnacles forever more enshrouded in sulpherous gloom under leaden skies of soot. Whilst the Mayor and Corporation claimed that what was coming would be artisans of the highest quality, craftsmen and artists of great skill working in wood and producing beautiful liveried paintwork on coaches. A sense of the William Morris idealism of the artist/craftsman was envisaged. Also it would enable the sons of working classes to learn a trade. The truth lay somewhere in between, not all the men would be highly skilled and the works would not be a gothic palace but a utilitarian structure sufficient unto the task at the right cost. In the event the GWR did not build the works at Oxford but built it at Swindon instead for £20,000 less. They considered the sites at Abingdon, Didcot and Reading too far from their town centres.

Chairman Richard Potter resigned and his successor, Daniel Gooch, dropped the Oxford plan altogether.

A poster of the time cites the traditional opposing interests of Town and Gown, that the University applied a great deal of pressure to oppose the plan, whilst local traders supported it as trade was desperately poor during University vacations. The author of the poster takes strong issue that the Uni-

Broad gauge 4-2-2 'Dragon' at Maidenhead on an 'up' train prior to 1890.
Laurence Waters Collection

versity was always making decisons and manipulating the destiny of Oxford to its own ends. The general feeling expressed at the time was that normally the University pays little attention to anything beyond the walls of Pembroke College, the nearest College to the railway at that time.

However, the GWR had much to gain from the University. Oxford station, during the end and beginning of term time handled 4,000 trunks and 800 bicycles, as stations go perhaps the only parallel would be Cambridge. The activity at the station at these times must have had all the animated assemblage of a University publication cartoon with impatient trains eager to escape in any and every direction.

All of this bearing in mind that in the 1950's the station was already running 152 passenger trains, 28 fish, parcel and empty stock trains on each weekday. On Saturdays this became 180 passenger and 23 others, about half being long distance expresses. The sixty locomotives held at Oxford depot would doubtless be well pressed into service with a virtually empty shed in the middle of the day.

In that elegent period of Armstrong and William Dean, with the large single wheel locomotives, before the First World War, the GWR were running 7ft 'singles' through Oxford on the Birmingham to London expresses of the 2-2-2 'Cobham' and 'Sir Alexander' classes with loads of seven or eight bogie coaches. Engine no 1128 'Queen' class 2-2-2 'Duke of York' was operating from Oxford until 1914. Owing to the smaller turntables on the northern section, shorter wheel base locomotives took the trains on from Oxford during this period.

In 1921 the longest through-coach working in British railway history passed through the station between Aberdeen and Penzance calling at Edinburgh, York, Sheffield, Nottingham, Leicester using the Woodford - Banbury link; Oxford, Swindon, Bristol, Exeter and Plymouth to Penzance totalling 785 miles. With all the crew and locomotive changes of different companies the headboard must have read as much as an adventure as a train journey!

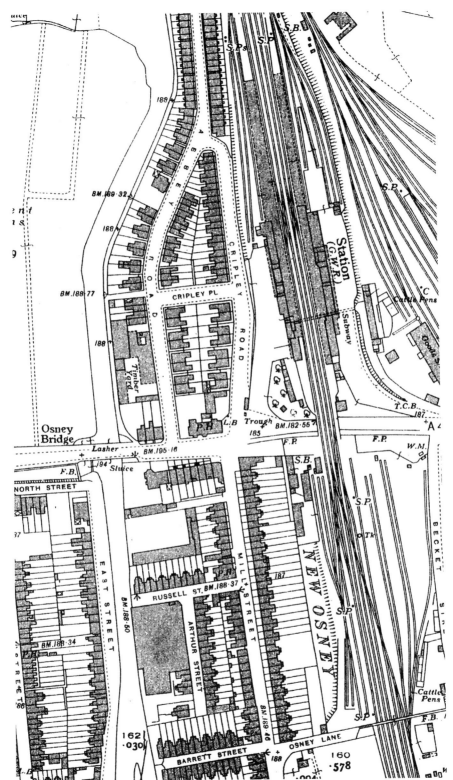

Layout of lines at Oxford in 1937 after the rebuilding of the station from the one demolished in the late 1870's. The lines fanning out right are for the former LNWR station from Cambridge and Bletchley. Note Osney Lane that was originally severed by the railway with a level crossing. When the GWR quadrupled the main line and added Becket Street sidings in 1866 this had to be replaced with a footbridge.

Reproduced by kind permission of Ordnance Survey Crown Copyright NC/01/479

The Goods yard at Oxford in 1934, before the distant gasworks.
Brunel University, Mowat, Clinker, Wookey, Locomotive Collection

Oxford station in the late fifties with 9F 2-10-0 92137 and West Country 4-6-2 34028. On the left a dmu in the early chevron or 'cats whisker' livery. Note the ornamental lampost on the left, a delightful piece of railway elegance.

Laurence Waters Collection

Locomotive 'Earl Baldwin' no 5063 at Oxford on the 11.00 am Hereford - Paddington train on February 27, 1954.
R J Buckley

One of the most significant features of railway development in Oxfordshire was the building and opening of the Manchester, Sheffield & Lincolnshire Railway's London extension from Annesley to Marylebone in 1899, renaming the company the Great Central Railway. The GCR formed a working relationship with the GWR for a new, shorter route to London avoiding Oxford. For this they established the GWR/GCR Joint Committee. This would remove some trains from the city station but, equally, brought much traffic to it with the construction of the Culworth Junction to Banbury North line of 1902 which proved such a valuable connection for through workings to the south and east midlands and the north. The Newcastle - Bournmouth via York, for example.

This contributed to a fascinating variation of trains at Oxford, particularly, in the summer months between the industrial north and the south coast resorts. In this situation the Southern engines came off their trains at Oxford to be replaced with the GWR going on to the GWR sheds to turn. Engines from the north GCR, later LNER, would do the same. Such well known trains for this were Bradford - Poole; York - Bournmouth; Bournmouth - Manchester (Pines Express) lately having completed its climb through the rolling Mendips until the Somerset & Dorset was closed and it was re-routed; also the Leicester - Southampton which saw GWR locos entering Leicester. Another was the Manchester - Banbury - Oxford - Reading - Guildford - Redhill and Dover with GCR coaches.

There was also a Newcastle - Southampton service that ran via Reading West loop on the south journey and via Newbury on the northward run and once included a through coach to Edinburgh (Waverley), a dining car that was attached at Oxford. One passenger train in the thirties that passed over GWR metals but was not hauled by a GWR loco was the Ashford - Newcastle. It continued between Reading and Banbury hauled by a three-cylinder Southern Mogul where it was handed over to a former GCR loco, a B7 4-6-0 as LNER. The train was sixteen bogies of LNER stock.

A superb study of a 4-4-0 no 3256 'Guinevere' entering south of Oxford station on July 10, 1933. 'The Duke of Cornwall' class originally sixty engines that were built between 1895 and 1899. Constructed for the hilly routes of the west country.

L Hanson

Due to intense freight activity as a result of the former GCR connection, goods sidings were extended north of Oxford in 1931. A new 'hump' marshalling yard was being built at Banbury at the same time.

Much of all of this was to prove so valuable with the outbreak of the Second World war and Oxford was concentrated with freight activity as the route mentioned reached the intensity it had known during the First World War. Added to this was the new freight line avoiding London route which brought connections north of Oxford with the LMS to Bletchley and a connection with the Southern at Reading. Much of the freight from the south was run straight into Hinksey Sidings which opened in 1942 when the Oxford North yard was found unable to cope. Hinksey Yard continued until 1967 when the system of marshalling trains ended. Sidings were also built at Moreton

Oxford station had been in poor condition for some time and was sheduled for rebuilding in the thirties, the last rebuild had taken place in 1891.

The war deferred all rebuilding of stations and infrastructure but like the other station at Banbury rebuilding was long overdue by the time it came in 1969. The ground beneath the station had always been of poor load bearing quality and during this rebuild it was extensively reinforced. The platform on the 'down' side was given an extension to the canopy of 150ft which had to be supported on piles.

On August 1, 1972 the new station buildings at Oxford were opened. These had cost £250,000 and presented a modern clean appearance to the travellers, in keeping with the seventies. A considerable improvement on the former buildings modified at the latter part of the nineteenth century but, that being said, the new buildings were grossly inadequate for a city like Oxford, more appropriate perhaps for a small town. Nevertheless they remained until they were replaced with new buildings twenty years later, the present structures, which whatever shortcomings does give greater circulating area. This new station was started in 1989

Entrance to Oxford station in the early Fifties.

Oxfordshire County Council Photographic Archive

costing £3 million. Rory Coonan in the *Observer* likened it to the the average DIY superstore and a complete design failure. This may well be a valid criticism but for anyone using the station compared to the former, just to have some space was a gain, be it less aesthetically utilised.

Oxford station enamel signs were taken down when the station was repainted in 1976.

The Act for the first Gas Company at Oxford received the Royal Assent on May 23, 1818. Situated on the banks of the Thames enabled coal to be delivered by barges on the Thames Navigation. The first works in St Ebbes was a modest affair by comparison with its later development and only supplied the nearest parts of the city. A further Act was acquired in 1869 to extend supply to Headington, St Clements, St Giles, Cowley, Iffley, St Aldate's, North Hinksey, South Hinksey and Botley. This required further expansion of the works on its situation on the north bank of the Thames.

A bridge was authorised in 1866 over the Thames to give access for the railway and a considerable expansion of the works on that side with large gasholders. A connecting foot-bridge was also built which remains in use.

Throughout the twentieth century the original site was dwarfed by development on the south side.

In 1892 the works were enlarged yet again to include gas supply for all of the city as far as Wolvercote. In 1924 the supply reached Abingdon and in 1930 absorbed the Abingdon Gas, Light & Coke Co Ltd. In 1932 this was extended to include Didcot. This brought the Company to the title of the Oxford and District Gas Company.

The works had two miles of railway sidings with its own locomotives and wagons. Also with two engine sheds, one on each side of the river, in the old and new works. Coal was mechanically tipped into feed hoppers and during the heavy winter period a full train load of coal each day would be brought into the works, about seven hundred tons.

The University brought pressure to bear so that the works was unable to develop business in the residual by-products from the manufacture of gas. Development of north sea gas brought closure in 1960.

In 1892 Oxford received its first electricity supply, with the opening of the generating works at Osney

Above: Oxford gasworks and sidings. Below: the huge gasholders that dominated the station area for many years on the south side of the river. The railway bridge was built to connect the south side with the original gasworks site on the north side of the river. All have of course gone now but the place can be compared as the bridge is still used as a footpath.

Oxfordshire County Council Photographic Archive

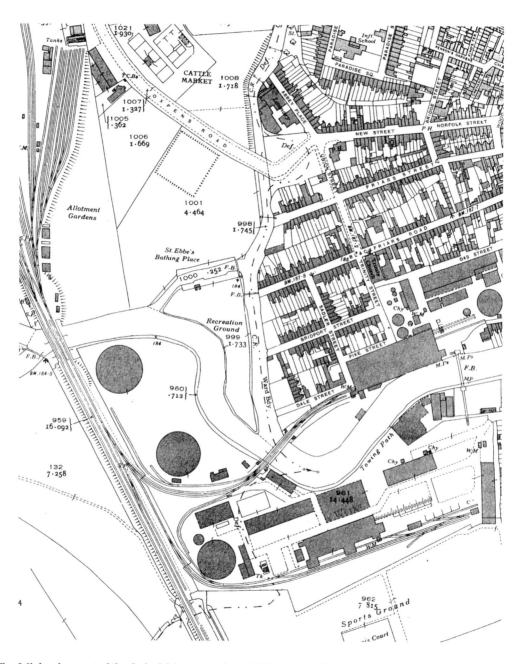

The full development of the Oxfordshire gasworks in 1939. It was self contained with its own railway system.
Reproduced by kind permission of Ordnance Survey Crown Copyright NC/01/479

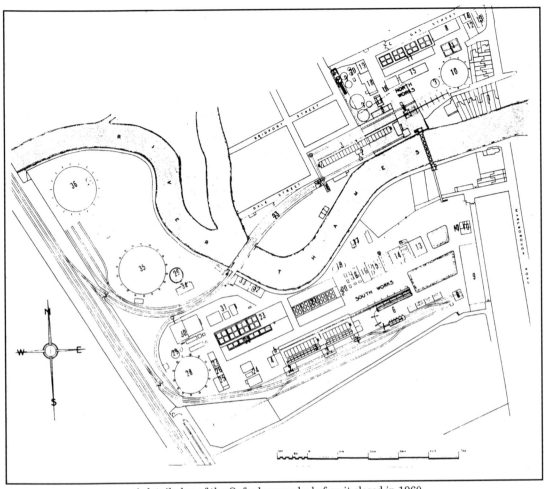

A detail plan of the Oxford gasworks before it closed in 1960

W G Bagnell Ltd 0-4-0 OC saddle tank of Oxford Gas Co no 1839, built in 1906 as a new engine to Oxford. This loco was employed at the old works site. It was scrapped on site by T Warburton (Oxford) Ltd in January in 1949

Frank Jones

Andrew Barclay Sons & Co Ltd 0-4-0 OC saddletank at the Oxford Gas Co. named 'Dover', this loco worked at the south new works site.

Frank Jones

W G Bagnell Ltd no 2656/42 0-4-0 OC saddle tank of Oxford Gas Co. Added as a new engine to Oxford working in the old works site in 1942. Odd locomotives that look like narrow gauge built for standard gauge track. This locomotive was scrapped on site by James Friswell & Son Ltd, Banbury in 1960.

Frank Jones

View south from Oxford station in the 1950's a Great Western 'Hall' is passed by former LNWR 0-8-0 freight engine in all possibility from Hinksey yard over to the Oxford - Bletchley line.

Laurence Waters

Oxford station no 1 platform in the late fifties, evidently 3.00 clock in the afternoon as 7912 'Little Linford Hall' arrives with the York - Bournmouth. The atmosphere of the old Oxford station exemplifies the period well with platform trolleys, gas lamps and weighing machines.

S Boorne

In the early sixties two former GWR pannier tanks probably returning from shunting work at Cowley heading into Oxford and the sheds.

Brian Sessions

The Osney Lane footbridge was a well used vantage point to view the trains south of Oxford. Here a 'West Country' pacific no 34103 'Calstock' of the Southern Region leaves Oxford passing the goods shed in the early sixties.

Brian Sessions

A 'Lord Nelson' class 30861 'Lord Anson' has just taken over the 9.35 am Birkenhead-Bournemouth train. Departure from Oxford was at 2.25 pm travelling via Reading West curve and Basingstoke. The Southern engine worked from Bournmouth shed to arrive at Oxford at 12.49 to coal and water and pick up the return working seen here.

R. J. Buckley

A view from the box as tank engine rolls into Oxford with freight from Morris Cowley. Note the long footbridge across the lines that had to be built in 1867 to continue Osney Lane that was originally a level crossing.

Laurence Waters

Class 25 diesel no 25218 passing the Oxford goods yard July 28, 1977.

Geoff Gamble

The numerous engine changing routines were a popular feature at Oxford with enthusiasts. The rich variety of different companies' engines acheived greater curiosity when the indigenous Brunswick Green could be compared with the sanguinity of the Midland Red! Here the Midland compound 1000 exchanges roles with the GWR Mogul on September 9, 1960.

Ken Fairey

One of the hydraulic Hymek locomotives D7056 heading south from Oxford in the early Sixties and likely to be a working from the Hereford, Worcester trains to Paddington upon which they were a common sight for much of their short life.

Brian Sessions

Engine no 6998 'Burton Agnes Hall', ready for the last steam locomotive run to Banbury, at Oxford.

Bruce Coleman

Typical of the problematic intensity at Oxford in steam days with all lines blocked with locomotives, either arriving or leaving. Note the parked auto coach on the right. Also on the left the fireman of the GWR engine takes advantage of a lull at signals to push some of the coal forward from the top of the tender.

Brain Sessions

Our Working Lives

Bruce Coleman

Fireman

'I started in 1964 as a cleaner at Oxford shed but they were so short of fireman that I was promoted in a week! So I went to do a fireing course up in Reading, I also did the signalling and train working courses. I stayed at Oxford shed and lasted until a year after steam ended when I was made redundant, not the career prospect that it had been by a long shot.

Nevertheless in that time I did see something of the local railway scene at its end. We had regular trips up to the car works and met 'Cheddar' Wilson who operated the engine there, he was an ex-British Railways man.

Funny thing up there, once when we came in to do an evening shift there was a place where the siding crossed the road and when we came to it they had tarmaced all the road and completely covered the rails. I was mystified but my driver said 'oh, don't worry, the engine will soon find its way', and it did.

In those days we still had a two-day shift with the pick-up goods over to Princes Risborough. We set off first calling at Littlemore, there was a turntable on the sidings for the hospital and we used to shunt a wagon on this and pinch bar it onto the hos-

pital siding. There was also petrol sidings at Littlemore so we would leave wagons off for that.

We would then call at Cowley with assorted wagons and shunt coal in the yard. Sometimes we had very heavy rolls of steel on bogie bolster wagons. To do this working, we would usually have a 61XX but occasionally a pannier and I have known it be a Black Five or 8 Freight.

The big problem was that when you came off the main line at Kennington Junction, you had to pick up the single line token and you couldn't slow down much for it because it was a sharp curve and a steep gradient, bearing in mind that you had the weight of these bolsters of steel. So the driver would go round as fast as he could and it was a nightmare worrying about this token, expecially in the dark, even though there was a weak beam of light from the lamp.

'Cheddar' Wilson with his diesel shunter would have his freight ready to come out onto our sidings which we unlocked.

On from there the next call was Wheatley and shunting. Wheatley would take at least an hour, coal and timber and such.

Then on to Tiddington and Thame and finally to Princes Risborough which would mean that we had been working twelve or thirteen hours by the time we got there. This meant an overnight stop at Risborough in the engineman's hostel. Next morning we set off to return repeating in reverse all that was needed for the Oxford direction.

What I liked at Oxford was the diversity of engines working into and out of shed. Great Western, of course, but also BR Standard types, old LNWR engines from Bletchley and the Southern engines as well, particularly the 'Merchant Navys'. You picked up the shovel on these engines and they gained ten pounds of steam immediately; beautiful engines to work on. We had a night parcels, about ten o'clock, to Wolverhampton and we often did it with a 'Merchant Navy' sometimes with a 'Britannia' or 9F 2-10-0.

Another working then was the 'Warships' up the Abingdon branch to pick up MG cars. Also quite a few box vans going into the goods shed and a heck of a lot of coal.

Finally I was rostered to work the very last steam working from Oxford the 2.10 pm to Banbury, which was to be a local engine, 'Burton Agnes Hall'. Fireman, Mick Cook, was going to be on it but he went sick that day and I was spare man.

I had a terrible job trying to get steam because there were so many dignatories around and they crowded the footplate so that I could not swing my shovel. I asked them politely to stand back so that I could get started which they reluctantly did, only to move again when I had put a few shovels full of coal on. Must have thought it was like a car that only needed a few squirts of petrol! And I needed to have them out of the way for an hour whilst I got the head of steam that was required. I was all the time trying to sneak a few shovels full on between the people. The result was that it was nowhere near as good a fire as it should have been and it was a heavy job all the way to Banbury.

One nice touch was that the nameplates had gone, they had been sold, so one of the boilermakers made up a new set of plates then cut out the letters from plywood and 'fretted' them by hand. It was so good that you had to get quite close to see that it was not the genuine article.

The Oxford shed was very atmospheric, dark and prevailing with odours of present and absent engines. When you went in there starting a shift at 2 o'clock in the morning it

Bruce with the Mayor of Oxford
Bruce Coleman

would be very quiet. The fire raiser would have lit the fire for you but you would have your preparation to do, three quarters of an hour on a tank engine, an hour on a tender. It was gloomy and wonderful, all at the same time . You thought about the years of comings and goings, of all the men that had done the same job as you were doing then down through the years and the wonderful engines that they had prepared.

To get paid you had a brass GWR token which you exchanged for your wage packet.

We had one shift of twelve hours on shed receiving engines coming in and getting others ready for the road. And, very often, the steam pressure was very low and the brakes did not work all that well and my driver and I would take turns to move an engine whilst the other would have a cup of tea. However my driver was moving an engine and pulled the lever to put the brakes on and it gently continued on to the turntable where the front bogie dropped down the well. So they got on to Swindon, this was at ten o'clock at night and by three in the morning the breakdown crane had arrived with a huge crane all steamed up and the engine was lifted, the bogies squared up on the rails and nothing went on the records at all.'

Locomotive 4061 'Glastonbury Abbey' at Didcot on a Stephenson Locomotive Society special from Birmingham to Swindon on September 11, 1955.

R J Buckley

CHAPTER 2

DIDCOT

The town of Didcot was not in Oxford shire until the boundary changes of 1974, which also included Abingdon and Wantage. Therefore in the interests of historical completeness they have been included in this study of the railways of south Oxfordshire. The newly formed GWR Company at that time comprised of two Committees respectively, meeting in London and Bristol. Steventon, near Didcot, being half way was chosen for full board meetings. Brunel was instructed to make extensive alterations to a house at Steventon that was used by the Superintendent of the Line. This house virtually became the seat of power of the GWR for six months from July 1842 to January 1843. After that time the two committees were abolished and a single board met in London. Interestingly the house was in the Tudor style which was very much the style favoured by Brunel for buildings on the line.

When the Steventon station was opened it gave railway access to all the nearby towns including Oxford which must have made it a very busy place indeed with coaches congregating to meet trains. For seven weeks it was the terminus of the main line until the section to Challow was ready.

Steventon was to return to its former repose as the concentration of railway business shifted a little east to the nearby village of Didcot where a new station was opened on the same day as the line to Oxford. Didcot was not however to be a railway mayfly but develop into a substantial railway operating centre.

In 1854 the GWR built new terraced houses near the station at Station Hill adding to these in 1904. The following year the Great Western Junction Railway Hotel was opened. Didcot was rapidly becoming a town as a result of the railway. A new Corn Exchange, near the station, was opened on October 20, 1857, this was gratifying to local growers with the railway giving them speedy access to London markets.

Didcot gained prominence with the opening of the railway to Oxford and a locomotive steam shed was built with brick walls and timber and slated gable style roof. It was 130ft by 50ft and opened in July 1857, to supply motive power for this branch and its proposed extensions on the north side of the station. This lasted until June 1932 when not only greater facilities were needed, but the land would be better serving for goods sidings and a new shed was built nearby on the site of the old carriage sheds. It was financed from the Loans & Guarantees Act of 1929 to ease unemployment and help update plant of ageing industries after the Great War. By 1935 this shed was allocated with forty-three locomotives and had a 65ft turntable. It was last used by British Rail in June 1965 and is now part of the complex of the Didcot Railway Centre (GWS).

Resourcefully the GWR built and opened a gas producing plant within the boundary of the original broad gauge locomotive shed, at the rear of the coal stages. It supplied gas for the engine shed, lighting around the area of the station and shunting yard. It also supplied gas for coach lighting.

Didcot's central position on the GWR system was confirmed when they opened their horse provender store inside the triangle in 1884, gathering grain and distributing it to their thousands of working horses. This enormous structure was like a northcountry mill, a remorseless domination of brick enclosing several floors and lifts supplying all the Company's thousands of horses with fodder. It had some standard gauge sidings and its own departmental loco no 4178 that was scrapped at Swindon in 1960. Its essential role ceased with motorisation and it was finally closed in 1953. From then on it was used by private firms for ten years until even this use ceased and it was finally demolished in 1976 and the area became the station car park.

An east curve avoiding the station, which was still in broad gauge, was installed in 1860 to allow north - south running of 1 mile 2 chains length. Narrow gauge rails were not put in at Didcot station until 1863.

Reading station was not mixed until April 1869. The avoiding line was put in as a result of the Shrewsbury Amalgamation Act promised by the Board of Trade in 1846 to allow trains between Wolverhampton and the London & South Western Railway, therefore there had to be a narrow gauge connection between Birmingham and Basingstoke.

By May 1872 narrow gauge rails had been laid between Didcot, Swindon, Gloucester and South Wales. In 1874 they were extended to Exeter. Eventually on May 21 and 22, 1892 the broad gauge was removed altogether beyond Exeter.

Further development was added with the opening on April 12, 1882 of the Didcot, Newbury & Southampton Railway to Newbury. This situation now required the rebuilding of the original station, which when completed, disasterously caught fire on March 11, 1886. Neverthless the importance of Didcot could not be forstalled by this happening and the work was undertaken again. One year later it was completed and Didcot had the station that is familiar to this day. This station had the necessary but unpopular means of access to trains between platforms along a subway. This was done both here and at Oxford and they became oppressive, fearsome places, poorly lit and dirty, wet and slimey. Changing trains, especially in the least populous hours must have been an ordeal of darkness.

To facilitate the building of a west curve required the purchase of Vauxhall House and farm buildings that were demolished after purchase in 1884. The connection to the main line at this point became known as Foxhall Junction (Vauxhall). It was opened on February 15, 1886.

This created an enormous triangle enclosing the GWR transfer shed for goods between the broad and 'narrow' gauge, a monument to the failed aspirations of Brunel's grand scheme. He would have dipped his pen in vitriol to draw plans for that! It was erected in 1863 when the GWR had mixed gauge on the Paddington - Birmingham line but broad only to Bristol. Therefore it was required to move goods from one line to another by a crane under cover. When the mixed gauge progressed to the west its purpose became defunct. The shed is the sole survivor of its type, there were ten, built entirely in timber and is 207ft long, 37ft wide and 30ft high. The roof has diagonal wooden braces. In the con-

East of Didcot station around the turn of the century, note the provender store in the distance. Interesting and somewhat unique is the view of the first broad gauge locomotive shed that can be seen on the right.

Laurence Waters

tracting world of British Rail when most things regardless of importance were dismissed by demolition, the shed found a safe haven at the nearby Didcot Railway Centre site where it authentically encloses broad gauge rails

Further traffic demands came with the opening of the Ministry of Munitions Depot and Arsenal in 1915. This was situated in an obviously advantageous position on the west curve at an important junction with lines going to the four points of the compass. This became the main Ordnance Supply Depot. Interestingly the army's main supply depot at the present is still in Oxfordshire with rail access at Bicester. An RAF depot was opened also.

Block section working was introduced on the line from Paddington to Bristol and to Oxford by March 1874. The station at its peak required six signalboxes to operate it, these were Didcot North, a new box was installed on July 16, 1905 with all points and signals powered by electricity, Siemans equipment this replaced two mechanical boxes. It reverted back to mechanical working in 1927. Other boxes were Didcot East End, Didcot East Junction, Didcot West Curve, Didcot West End and Foxhall Junc-

tion. Still further on due to the expanding traffic the quadrupling of the main line between Taplow and Didcot began in the summer of 1890.

In 1930 the GWR announced that they were to extend their version of Automatic Train Control, this was installed at that time from Paddington to Oxford but no further north. It was then extended to Banbury and Worcester, also the Fairford and Henley branches.

The system gives audible warning to the driver of signals ahead and in the event of this being ignored it will automatically stop the train.

The concentration of movements at large railway junctions was bound to result in many accidents. The marvel is, that with such intensive movements around a busy main line area that there were in fact so few. These are some involving Didcot:

On January 6, 1932 engine 2949 'Stanford Court' working a 'down' milk empties ran into the engine of a goods train at Didcot East Box at 3.25 am. The engine fell on her side smashing ten wagons and damaging seventeen others. On March 27, 1935 driver Ernest Edmonds was fatally crushed when his engine that he was oiling inside 3254 'Cornubia' was bumped by 4917 'Crosswood Hall'. In the

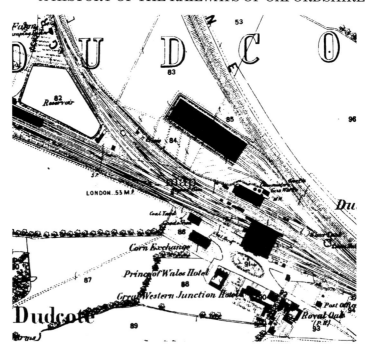

Didcot in 1875 note the corn exchange established as a result of the arrival of the railway. Note also reservoir on site of later provendor store.

Reproduced by kind permission of Ordnance Survey Crown Copyright NC/01/479

dark days of World War II, November 13, 1942 engine 2975 'Lord Palmer' working a coal train, unusual for the large driving wheel 'Saint', was routed down the Goods Loop to Appleford. Unfortunately the driver mistook a signal for the main line to be for him, the result was that he was derailed at the catch points and the engine finished up on its side in a field with the tender on top of it. Tragically the fireman was killed instantly, the driver, who was scalded, died some hours later.

Of all the accidents taking place at Didcot the greatest tragedy was the derailment at speed of the Britannia Pacific no 70026 'Polar Star' that occured between Steventon and Didcot. It was on a ten coach excursion from Treherbert, South Wales to Paddington. It was derailed at about 1 pm on Sunday, November 20, 1955 at Milton. It had been diverted to the 'up' goods loop from the 'up' main line on which engineering works were in progress. It left the rails and went down the embankment bringing, and wrecking, the first four coaches with it. As a result ten persons were killed and ninety-six were taken to hospital. The driver and fireman were not

seriously hurt. At the official enquiry the driver admitted that he had overlooked the notice of a diversion and was travelling at about 50 mph. He claimed that he was on a strange engine with left hand drive and failed to observe the two signals on the approach to the loop. Rather alarmingly the fireman at the enquiry admitted that on another occasion he had overridden the ATC equipment which the crew were forbidden to do. They claimed that they did not hear the bell as the class was capable of excessive noise and the bell could be muffled by clogging dirt.

A petrol train crash took place on August 14, 1964 when 14 tank wagons overturned and caught fire damageing 300 yards of the London - Oxford main line. Part of the damage included the footbridge just north of the diverting lines at Didcot. The locomotive was 2-8-0 no 48734 which was cut up.

A northbound freight hauled by a class 47 D1775 became derailed at Foxhall Junction on January 1, 1966. No serious injury was caused but the Paddington to Bristol and South Wales line was blocked for while.

The inaugural meeting of the Great Western Society was held at Southall Community

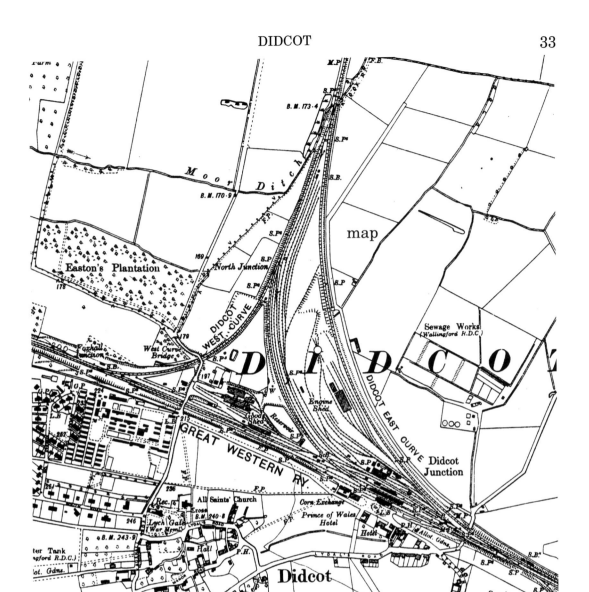

Didcot in pre-eminence, the important railway Junction of the Great Western Railway, this survey in 1928.
Reproduced by kind permission of Ordnance Survey Crown Copyright NC/01/479

Centre on Friday, May 4, 1961 between 8 pm and 10 pm. In consequent development the Society became established at Didcot in 1967.

The first acquisition of engines for the Society came with no 6106 in November 1967, which can still be seen at Didcot. Engine no 1466 was stored at Totnes 1964-67, arriving at Didcot in December 1967 whilst no 6998 'Burton Agnes Hall' came in December 1967. Engine 1340 'Trojan' arrived at Didcot in March 1968. The former Sandy & Potton and later Wantage Tramway well tank 'Shannon' was brought to Didcot in 1969. Whilst no 5051 'Drysllwyn Castle' came in February 1970. Followed by 0-6-2T, no 6697 in August 1970, also no 7808 'Cookham Manor' in Au-

gust 1970. Later engines were 4-6-0 5900 'Hinderton Hall' and 0-6-0 no 3650 pannier tank that arrived at Didcot in 1971 from Barry Scrapyard.

The locomotive works of the Great Western Society opened on Sunday, April 24, 1988.

At about the same time a signalbox from Frome was also erected on the site.

A new 150ft long carriage shed was built at Didcot in January-February 1977. As a result of a loan from the Manpower Services Commission the Society was able to employ twelve persons.

Three nearby stations also received improvements, Wantage Road, Challow and Shrivenham, by British Railways in 1972.

Didcot station looking east on July 17, 1933, obviously a quiet moment.
Brunel University, Mowat, Clinker, Wookey Locomotive Collection

The 'branch' to Oxford, July 17, 1933.
Brunel University, Mowat, Clinker, Wookey Locomotive Collection

Didcot station on June 17, 1933, in the distance right the newly built locomotive shed and coaling stage.
Brunel University, Mowat, Clinker, Wookey Locomotive Collection

Looking west at Didcot platform end with engine 2953 'Titley Court'. Note beyond, the GWR broad gauge transfer shed in use as a goods shed. This view August 16, 1936 shows the West End signalbox. A taste for elaboration with the early electric lamp design.

H C Casserley

Didcot in June 1932, activity on the platform on the platforms with building work being undertaken would be part of the building activity taking place all around the station at this time. The new locomotive shed would be part of this programme. The roof of the old one can be seen behind the signal on the right.

Brunel University / Mowat, Clinker, Wookey Locomotive Collection

Steventon, the station that began trains in Oxfordshire.

Laurence Waters Collection

A GWR 'Saint' 2903 'Lady of Lyons' passing old and new West End signalboxes on August 21, 1932. The new box was opened in December 1931 and was closed in may 1965.

L Hanson

Steventon early this century looking towards the west. The neat and tidy appearance of the railway in this period ascends to an art of perfection.

Laurence Waters Collection

Contrast of the ages, Steventon station with a train passing through hauled by one of the short lived diesel hydraulic classes a 'Warship'. Picturesquely Steventon reflects the early days of the line. One can easily imagine the assemblage of dozens of omnibus coaches and carrier carts in the space on the right beyond the station buildings. Whilst behind is the house where the early separate committees of the Great Western Railway met and deliberated on the fortunes and prospects of their new line, along with their courageous engineer Isambard Kingdom Brunel.

Laurence Waters

A train on the avoiding loop at Didcot, passing the locomotive sheds, hauled by ex-GWR 4-6-0 7000 'Viscount Portal' on July 25, 1963.

Laurence Waters

A train of coal hoppers on the west side avoiding line, hauled by 2-8-0 8F 48762 in the early Sixties .

Brian Sessions

The prototype 2,800hp diesel-electric locomotive D0280 (1200) 'Falcon' was built at Loughborough works by Brush Electrical Engineering Co Ltd. in 1961. It worked the 'Sheffield Pullman' from King's Cross after, as seen here, undergoing successful trials on the Western Region where it hauled light train loads of 273 tons which allowed it to reach 100 mph on the level and 75 mph when hauling a train of 600 tons (18 vehicles). On the Lickey incline which is 1 in 37.7 the loco started smoothly from a standstill with a load of 628 tons (20) vehicles.

On the Western Region main line west of Newton Abbot, where there are gradients of 1 in 36 to 1 in 47 on severe curves, smooth starting was acheived on the worst sections with 568 tons. The locomotive acheived 120,000 miles in 18 months of extensive testing. It was classified singularly as class '53' but was the precursor of the most successful general purpose locomotive on British Railways the 'Class 47'.

The locomotive was finally delivered to British Railways Western region in 1965 and painted in the standard colours but retained its 'Falcon' emblem. It was reported to be working from the Bristol Bath Road depot. It left Ebbw Junction shed and arrived for scrapping at Cashmore's Yard, Newport, on March 28, 1976.

Brian Sessions

An advancing 'Warship' passes the broad gauge transfer shed in the 1960's.

Laurence Waters Collection

Apparent aid for class D1752 from 6995 'Benthall Hall' at Didcot in the early Sixties with a very modest train. Behind is Didcot West End signalbox

Brian Sessions

Moreton Cutting in 1952 looking towards Didcot with AEC diesel railcar passing through. The GWR introduced streamlined AEC railcar with 130hp engine to operate services between Swindon, Didcot, Oxford, Princes Risborough, Witney and Banbury. Later cars had lower and better windows and a sliding door instead of a swing open door. By 1936 the GWR were operating 55 streamlined railcar services daily on their system although there were only eighteen vehicles in number, including a parcels car, they worked from ten sheds, serving 247 stations.

The first car was introduced in February 1934 and had a gearbox as used by London buses.

In 1935 three cars were introduced to Oxford, followed by ten in 1936. The parcels car worked from the depot of J. Lyons & Co Ltd at Addison Road to Reading and Oxford then returned to London. They had two AEC Ricardo 6-cylinder 130 hp oil engines with a normal speed of 1,850 rpm. These were fitted with an independent drive to either bogie on each side of the chassis.

All controls except the throttle were pneumatically operated, air for this purpose was provided by two small compressors mounted one on each engine. The throttle was operated mechanically as it was necessary to use this when starting up the engine and before a supply of compressed air was available.

Brian Higgins

The establishment of the GWR Society, Didcot Railway Centre on the site of the locomotive steam shed at Didcot in the mid sixties provided the county with a lasting reminder of the railway that served it so well for many years. Many engines went to the scrapyards throughout the Fifties and Sixties but, at Didcot it is still possible to see representatives of the various classes and recall memories of the times when they were commonly and affectionately regarded. This view in September 1971 shows prominently 0-6-2T no 6697, note the east curve behind.

C R L Coles

Former LMS loco 46251 'City of Nottingham' on a visit with an RCTS special in 1964.

Brian Sessions

A splendid presentation of the 'Bulldog' engine no 3454 'Skylark' on a bright sunny June 17, 1951 as it leaves
Didcot with a train for Swindon to Birmingham chartered by the Stephenson Locomotive Society.

R J Buckley

A good view of the broad gauge transfer shed in situ with visiting engine T9 of the Southern Region having just
arrived at Didcot with a Newbury and Southampton train on March 26, 1959.

B W L Brooksbank

Didcot locomotive shed in the early sixties. It came under the London Division of the GWR as 'DID'.
Brian Sessions

G. W. R. Station, Wantage Road.

Wantage Road early this century, the station for the resourceful Wantage Tramway. The station was opened in 1846 and was extensively rebuilt in 1934 as a result of additional loop lines.
Lauerence Waters Collection

Brian Sessions

Engine no D1775 class 47 that became derailed at Foxhall Junction with a north bound freight on January 1, 1966. Below: an alarming prospect for the signalman! The box had closed by this time and was soon removed altogether.

Brian Sessions

The ascent of main line running, light engine 34026 'Yes Tor' being passed by two three-car sets dmu in early 'chevron' livery. Also about to be overtaken by a 'Western' hydraulic heading towards London.

Brian Sessions

The broad gauge transfer shed in situ on the Didcot Railway Centre site authentically enclosing broad gauge track in the foreground.

Bill Simpson

Pannier tank no 3721 was fitted with a special spark arrestor chimney for working in and out of the Government stores at Didcot. The engine was withdrawn April 20, 1964 and cut up at Swindon on May 16, of the same year. Didcot Ordnance Depot trains ran in to a platform inside the depot from Banbury and Oxford during the war. This view August 16, 1947.

H C Casserley

A 9F 92033 2-10-0 pausing outside the Didcot horse provender stores in the early sixties.

Brian Sessions

Landscapes of power, the new power station was opened at Didcot in the mid 1960's with a continuous coal feed of trains on a 'merry-go-round system' between Toton yard in Nottinghamshire and Didcot. Various diesel types worked this cycle from pairs of class 20's to 47, 56, 58, 59, 60. Here a 47 has discharged its load and is turning in the loop to go back.

Laurence Waters

Early power station coal train at Oxford with class 20's

Laurence Waters

King Edward VIII no 6029 on the dead end siding in the 1960's, note the back of the huge provender store in the background.

Laurence Waters

Petrol train derailment at Didcot on August 14, 1964 when 2-8-0 48734 came off on the junction point of lines on the Oxford line north of Didcot. Note the damaged footbridge.

Brian Sessions

Black Five no 45493 crossing the bow string girder bridge at Appleford.

Brian Sessions

Bridge over the Thames at Nuneham.

Bill Simpson

Appleford Halt on November 27, 1983. This halt was opened in 1933. The original Appleford station on this location was opened in 1844 but closed in 1849. To this day the station retains its GWR pagoda platform shelters

Peter Baughan

Appleford

The first Appleford station was opened on the same day as the line on June 12, 1844 on milepost 55. The station appears to have had a very short life of only five years and closed in 1849.

By 1933 the population around Appleford increased sufficiently for the GWR to consider it viable to open a timber Halt at the same place on September 11, with tickets issued by a local agent, the post office. In later years they were issued from the train. The station was renamed Appleford Halt on May 5, 1964.

Close to Appleford is a bridge over the Thames of the bow-string girder type that was originally built in timber. It was rebuilt in steel about 1880 and rebuilt again in 1928.

Appleford Crossing signalbox was damaged in an accident on September 11, 1952.

Appleford crossing signalbox the original signalbox was demolished by a goods train in September, 1952.

Culham early last century, a small country station that could hardly be more attractive in representational Tudor. Its survival to this day is a unique railway architectural feature for Oxfordshire

Culham

Built with the opening of the Oxford branch carrying the names Dorchester Road and Abingdon Road until the opening of the Abingdon branch on June 6, 1856. Typical of the choice of Brunel who favoured the Tudor style for stations on the early Great Western Railway, built in brick with stone dressings. It also had a matching goods shed with pointed arch entrances. It remains to this day as a listed building, seeing modern diesel trains pass along platforms imbued with the memories of the early broad gauge trains. The station was further extended in 1909. The station closed to goods on July 19, 1965. Additional platforms have now been built alongside the old. It must be amongst the very few surviving small intermediate stations from 1844 in the country.

The Tudor style was splendidly repeated in the goods shed.

Culham looking towards Oxford in 1933 the detail of the building on the 'down' side can be viewed from this photograph.

Brunel University, Mowat, Clinker, Wookey Locomotive Collection

Abingdon Junction

Abingdon Junction station opened June 2, 1856 as an interchange point for passengers using the Abingdon branch and was closed with the opening of Radley station June 8, 1873.

Abingdon and Thame branches approaching Oxford, the original Abingdon Junction platform was at the junction of the Abingdon branch.

Bill Simpson Collection

Radley station change for the Abingdon branch which is the platform facing the camera. The short platform on the right was for horse boxes and milk traffic.

Radley

Radley station opened for passengers on September 8, 1873 replacing the Abingdon Junction station. The platforms were considerably extended between May 1948 to March 1949. As a passenger station it remains in use but closed to goods traffic on June 21, 1971. It was built to serve the village and as a new interchange point for the Abingdon branch. A little north of this point between mileposts $61\frac{1}{2}$ and $61\frac{3}{4}$ was Abingdon Road Halt which was opened in February 1908. Due to the wartime emergency it was closed March 22, 1915 and never re-opened.

Tank engine 72XX 7236 2-8-2 passing through Radley station on a freight train on September 9, 1961.

B K B Green

A splendid presentation of 2933 'Bibury Court' moving away briskly from Radley with a stopping train on May 15, 1948.

Laurence Waters Collection

Still proudly bearing the initials 'GWR' the 2-6-2 tank engine number unknown draws into Radley with a Didcot bound train in 1950.

Laurence Waters Collection

The remains of Hinksey Yard sidings in the 1970's with what appears to be one of the 'Merry-go-round' trains in storage. Note the ubiquitous brake van in the foreground, so much a part of the railway scene for many years until all stock became fully fitted.

Laurence Waters Collection

Hinksey Yard with 6998 'Burton Agnes Hall' passing by. Hinksey Yard was opened in 1942 as part of the freight diversionary route around London. It had twelve roads and was capable of holding 500 wagons.

Bill Simpson

Thame station in August 1962 with one of the 61XX class no 6149 on the 1.20 pm Oxford to Princes Risborough. There is a general feeling of emptiness and inactivity which fuelled the impending Beeching report on lines like Thame. Hard to argue against but sad to recognise, now that the great surge of road building was in its ascendancy.

R C Riley

CHAPTER 3

THAME BRANCH

The market town of Thame typifies the small towns of Oxfordshire that began very much as agricultural communities and later became partly industrialised with the continuing flexibility of manufacturing systems and, of course, transport that was developed by the railway. This continues with a road network now that the railway has gone.

The physical impact of the railway is largely confined within its boundaries whereas road development is free to sprawl wherever it will, bringing encroaching urbanisation, bypasses and the building of a main trunk motorway not far away. This presents a very different Thame from the one that saw the arrival of the broad gauge.

The entire route to Princes Risborough does, of course, extend into Buckinghamshire but for the sake of historical completeness the entire line is portrayed in this chapter.

This connecting branch of some twenty miles grew from the Buckinghamshire direc-

tion, a proposal was made by the Wycombe Railway that ran a branch from the GWR main line at Maidenhead, to extend to the market town of Thame some 12 miles 6 furlongs 8 chains in broad gauge in 1857. This single track line was built and opened on August 1, 1862 at a cost of £108,000. It was later extended, and opened, without ceremony, from Thame to Kennington Junction, some 13 miles, to connect with the line to Oxford from Didcot. Two intermediate stations at that time were Wheatley and Littlemore. This was opened on Monday, October 24, 1864. It began with four trains each way daily, doubtless with hope for development as it had cost some £150,000. It had filled an obvious gap between Oxford and Aylesbury which fortunately for the company was not filled with the proposed extension from Aylesbury by the London & Birmingham in 1840. The engineer for the line was one E F Murray.

The entire undertaking of the WR, some

The route of the Thame branch from Oxford to Thame based on an early survey that included Cowley but has had later modifications. Note the heavy climb over Shotover Hill and the tunnel. Brunel's scheme of 1854 would have taken the railway south of Shotover, thus avoiding a tunnel.

Author's Collection

44 miles in broad gauge, was amalgamated with the GWR, who had always worked the railway, on February 1, 1867.

The Thame line had been the first line to use the train staff and ticket system.

Interestingly the first survey for the line made in 1854 by I K Brunel, surveys the complete line to Oxford turning south after Thame and going further south of the village of Cuddesden, avoiding Wheatley, through Garsington, Blackbird Leys and then picking up the same route through Littlemore.

From August 23, to September 1, 1870 the entire line from the Junction at Maidenhead to Kennington Junction, 36 miles 58 chains was converted to the 'narrow' gauge.

The railway was commonly regarded as a useful cut-off or deviation from the Didcot route for traffic moving north and south to Paddington. It was, however, no real substitute for a main line railway although it was $7^{1}/_{4}$ miles shorter. It had gradients in places of 1 in 68 and a number of sharp curves at Risborough. Some of the bridges were not considered to be of the most robust construction and of course it was single track with a speed restriction of 10 mph between Wheatley and Horspath on a steep descent to Oxford. Nevertheless it was possible on occasions to witness a striking contrast from the humble branch tank engine and its two coaches when a 'Castle' 4-6-0 came by with its smart array of coaches with destination boards, the imposing pride of the GWR, rumbling by disproportionately through modest stations of a branch line.

Comparison of distances from Paddington is interesting, via Reading and Didcot it is

$63^{1}/_{2}$ miles to Oxford. A shorter route is via Denham, High Wycombe, Princes Risborough and Thame which was $55^{3}/_{4}$ miles when the branch was open. From Marylebone it was 57 miles. The distance from Euston to Oxford via Bletchley is 78 miles.

Between the junctions Thame was the major station of the line which at opening had a population of some 13,000. It is a substantial market town of many fine buildings, many of them in timber. The station building also in timber had an all-over roof Brunel style, similar to the one at Banbury (see Vol.1). The station itself was at the extreme eastern part of the town alongside the Thame Park Road. It had a large goods yard with four sidings situated on the 'up' side. Behind the 'down' platform is another siding on which extensive cattle pens were built, the GWR had to buy extra land in 1930 to accommodate them.

The railway had much its own way until 1922 when the City of Oxford Motor Bus Co introduced a service to Thame.

Traffic on the line was much developed with the introduction of an oil terminal at Thame in January, 1958 providing daily return workings.

The passenger service ceased to run on January 7, 1963 and the goods between Thame and Cowley ceased in 1965. The car works continues to use the part of the branch from Cowley but the oil terminal closed in the Nineties and the track has since been removed back to Princes Risborough. It is now a walkway and cycle path from Princes Risborough almost to the station site a Thame.

The signalbox at Kennington Junction in 1922. The box was installed with an electric key token post and set down post with net.

Lurence Waters Collection

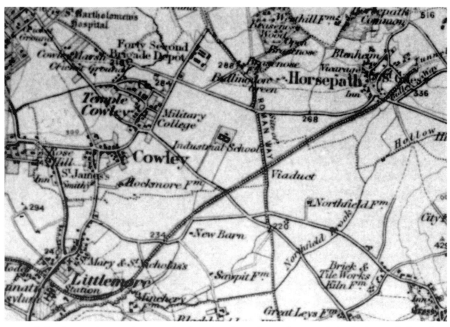

The area around Cowley in the 1860's, note the distance from the railway and the Military College building that was used to begin the enormous building impact of the motor car works that developed towards the railway.

Following the Thames towpath brings this remarakable bridge into view at Kennington. What a superb position to view the locomotives of Dean, Armstrong and Churchward in their days. This bowstring girder structure was opened in July 1923 to replace the deteriorating one of 1863. With one less support it also gave better clearance on the river. Here in the 1980's, diesel 31156 crosses with a car train. The Iffley Halt of 1908 was close by the bridge until it closed in 1915, for its short life at the convenience of the village of Kennington.

Laurence Waters

Kennington Junction

After just over two miles from Oxford a train for Thame and Princes Risborough would leave the main line at Kennington Junction and take its single track route through the gentle rolling landscape of rural Oxfordshire. Before the area became strung with road systems and roundabouts a journey out along this line, would be an experience, in terms of the unique way that railways aspired to to become part of the landscape, but not violate it. The countryside was able to accommodate a single set of rails in a way that it is difficult to imagine a six lane motorway with its unremitting roar and fumes would ever do. Therefore, from a carriage window, the view was as if one had a privileged seat to an undisturbed view of the landscape. The train could of course be seen and was noisey, but the imposition was as routine as the timetable, to the extent that grazing cattle grew to ignore it. A binding of brakes, a gentle hiss of steam, a porter's voice calling out his station's name, an exchange of pleasanteries between arriving or departing relatives and friends. These were station sounds that were part of that far off country of the past.

NEW RAIL MOTOR-CAR SERVICE.

To-morrow (Saturday) the Great Western Railway Company inaugurate the rail motor-car service that has long since been promised in the district. By this service considerable extensions will be made upon the existing passenger traffic between Shipton and Heyford on the north, and Princes Risborough, Thame and Wheatley on the south, while new districts will be opened up by the provision of "halts." These halts, which are stations in miniature, have been provided at Wolvercote, Hinksey (near the Waterworks), Abingdon-road (at the foot of Hinksey Hill), Iffley (between Kennington junction and Littlemore), Garsington Bridge (on the Cowley-Stadhampton-road), and Horspath village. For this service three rail motors and a "trailer" will be stationed at Oxford, and two will be continuously running. Two of these cars arrived at Oxford early in the present week, and a member of our staff was shown them by the courtesy of the station officials. The cars are substantially built, and appear to be of greater dimensions and power than those employed on the London and North Western Oxford-Bicester service. They are 74ft. long, and are divided into six compartments. At one end is the engine-room, rendered particularly spacious by the employment of a vertical type of boiler. Next to this is the luggage-van, and then the "smokers" compartment, with comfortable cane-upholstered seats, accommodating 22 persons. In the centre of the car is a small entrance vestibule, and next to this, remote from the engine, the principal compartment, similarly upholstered with longitudinally and latitudinally arranged seats, capable of comfortably accommodating 36 persons. At the far end of the car is the driver's cabin, permitting of dual control of driving and heating gear. The cars are lighted throughout by inverted incandescent gas burners, and are propelled by powerful machinery capable of maintaining a speed equivalent to that in the customary passenger service. It may be interesting, technically, to note that the driving

machinery is equipped with an American reversing valve motion, and, unlike that employed on the L. and N.W.R., is visible from outside. The cars weigh approximately 45 tons.

The service is, of course, primarily intended as a feeder to the more popular main-line trains, but will incidentally open up new traffic between Oxford and several villages. The first car of the day leaves Oxford between seven and half-past, and reaches Wheatley before eight. This returns in time for the 9.5 express to Paddington. The second car leaves Oxford for Bletchingdon shortly after eight and also returns in time for the 9.5 express. The car from Wheatley then passes on to Shipton, and that from Bletchingdon returns to Bletchingdon. The trips are then varied in distance, and two journeys are made each way between Oxford and Princes Risborough, cars leaving Oxford shortly after one and half-past four. In order that Blenheim and Woodstock may benefit by the new service an additional trip will be run on the Woodstock branch to Kidlington early each evening. Parcels will be conveyed between stations as by ordinary service, but not to and from halts. We understand that the fare from Oxford to Wolvercote will be 2d., similar to that charged by the L. and N.W.R. The fares in the other direction were not officially announced at the time of writing, but we understand they will possibly be: Oxford-Hinksey, 1½d.; Oxford-Abingdon-road, 2d.; Oxford-Iffley, 2½d.; Oxford-Garsington-road, 4d.; Oxford-Horspath, 5d.

Notice of the new railmotor service around Oxford in the *Oxford Times* February 1908.

Littlemore station looking towards Thame. The Lunatic Asylum on the right dominated the site. The siding to this building was accessed by a wagon turntable. Tragically, as described by Ken Bampton in volume one of this history, one of the inmates from the Asylum committed suicide on the line on his first day as signalman.

R M Casserley

Littlemore

The first station was for Littlemore with its single platform and two sidings, one of which was for the County Lunatic Asylum. This was reached via turntable in the goods yard which was probably for coal for heating the building which virtually dominated the site.

Towards Oxford a long siding ran parallel with the running line for about 500 yards. This served a petrol depot and some sand pits. The GWR purchased more land to extend this in 1914. Long sidings seem to have their own peculiar personality, too short for a branch but outgrowing their station bound companions, as they weave off into the countryside to find a source to tap for the railway company. When that source ceases to be fruitful, either by closure or alternative transport, their overgrown isolation adds to the melancholy of their plight. Which appears to have overtaken this siding about 1970.

The station had its own signal box which closed with the line in January 1963 and to goods in 1967.

The bow-string girder bridge across the Thames at Kennington on April 25, 1985. Note on the left on the opposite side of the river the abutment of the original bridge of 1863 that was replaced with the present structure in 1923.

Brian Higgins

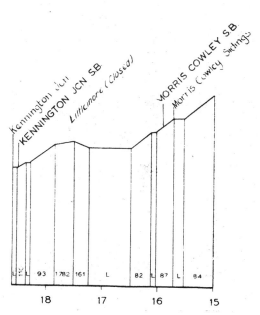

The steep climb from Kennington Junction to the tunnel near Wheatley over Shotover.

A timetable of 1862 for the Thame line

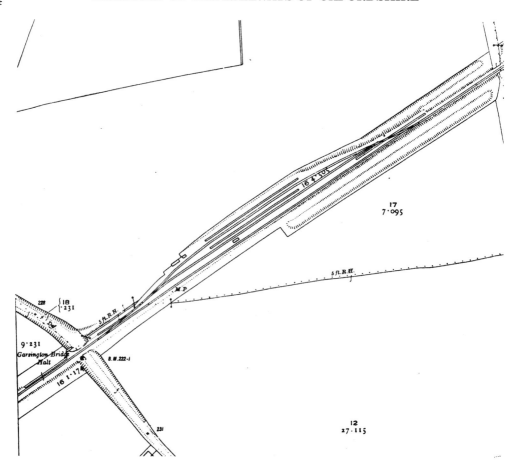

The first sidings at the subsequent site of the car works sidings. These were opened for the Ministry of Defence during the First World War when the works turned over to producing war materials including mine sinkers. A narrow gauge railway between the works and these sidings was also built. It was removed by 1922. Note Garsington Bridge Halt

Reproduced by kind permission of Ordnance Survey Crown Copyright NC/01/479

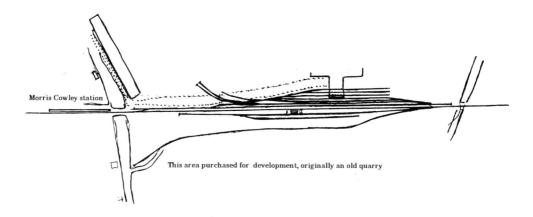

The sidings for the car works on the site in 1928, when expansion demanded the building of 50,000 square feet of transhipment shed alongside the rails. A proper entrance road was built at this time for the station.

Morris Cowley in 1932, note the single line. The signals are near the Garsington Road bridge. The area beyond was to become enormously developed by the car works with numerous sidings being added over the years
Brunel University, Mowat , Clinker, Wookey Collection

Morris Cowley

Morris Cowley, originally Garsington Bridge Halt, opened February 1, 1908

When the line reaches Morris Cowley it may seem somewhat in contrast with its rustic nature as the sidings and works access for the original Morris Motor Car works. But industry in Oxfordshire did not mean the same thing as industry in a large city. The original motor works though it grew to be dominant was removed in its isolation from the milieu of Oxford. Its many private sidings provided welcome business for the railway even though it would be transporting a contribution to its own downfall, the private car.

The first siding at this point Garsington Bridge, was put in during 1917. This was when the Trench Warfare Supply Department took over the works of Morris Motors for the production of castings (mine sinkers). For this a narrow gauge railway was built, of which some track remained in 1958.

After the war this became defunct and was later removed.

Garsington Bridge Halt, that was opened in 1908, was no more than a simple timber halt on the embankment with steps leading up from Garsington Road. The intention was to bring rail access to Cowley and Garsington. A Bill was submitted for the development of this Halt into a full station for the works in 1928.

The name Cowley was adopted from a suburb of Oxford, over a mile from the station. Morris was, of course, the name of the founder of the business William Morris, later Lord Nuffield, who opened his motor car business in 1912, Morris Motors Limited was founded in 1919.

In April 1913 the first Morris car, a two-seater 8.9hp costing £185, rolled off the production line and a new and important chapter in the history of Oxford was born.

Morris began to operate a private bus serv-

0-4-0 Diesel by John Fowler no 21456 built in 1937 for Linwood Works, Paisley, came to Cowley in 1938.

GWR Trust

ice between the station and the works as this original station was set in the open fields some distance away. But as the demands of the motor car business increased so did the works which came to absorb the land around the railway.

The works began their development from Temple Cowley in 1927 from the buildings that were once a military college and grew towards the railway where three sidings were laid on the 'up' side; also for the new associated works of Pressed Steel Fisher.

By 1928 traffic demands had increased so that a goods yard was laid down on the 'down' side and along with a new signalbox which was opened in September of that year. The passenger station became outstanding for its abundance of electric lights, whilst other stations on the line still used oil lamps.

The goods requirements increased so that the sidings on the 'up' were extended from three to six with broad end loading ramps being built at the end of two. A large corrugated iron goods shed was built and a driveway leading up to the passenger station. The station itself consisted of one platform and wooden buildings. Workmen's traffic was

catered for with a through train operating from Banbury that left at 6.00 am arriving at Cowley at 7.00 am. This began by terminating at Cowley but was later rostered to continue on to Princes Risborough. The return working left Cowley at 5.08 pm and reached Banbury at 6.06 pm. On Saturdays it left at 12.10 pm and ran to Kingham with a connection to Banbury from Kingham. A railmotor from Ascot-under-Wychwood serving the Worcester line connected with the morning train in Oxford.

Apart from the conveyance of the finished products from the works, there was the supply of raw materials and coal to contend with. Whilst a steady supply of bricks were brought down through Oxford from the Oxford to Cambridge line which was linked by sidings to dozens of London Brick Company factories.

Cars ran to Brentford for export, reversing at Kennington Junction, whilst a daily train ran from Bordesley with car bodies. Later a container and car loading depot was built for the use of MAT Transport on the site of the coal sidings. This was for loading containers of motor car parts and for load-

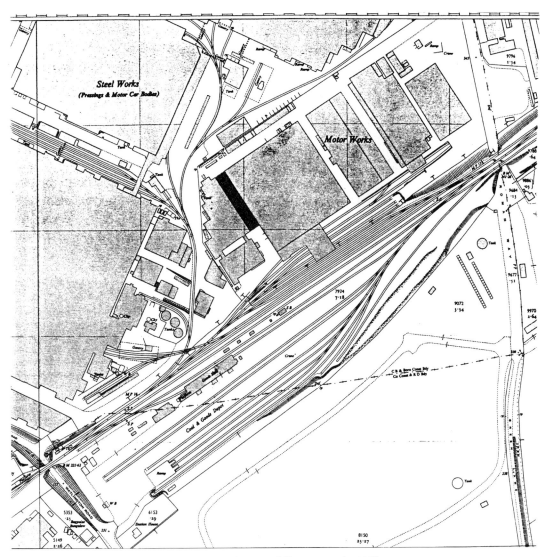

The car works at its fullest extent in 1955
Reproduced by kind permission of Ordnance Survey Crown Copyright NC/01/479

ing completed cars onto Cartic 4 double deck car transporters. What was originally the Stationmaster's house was later converted to an office.

In 1930 the GWR announced that, owing to increasing demand at Birmingham and Oxford, a 100 special design trucks were to be built for the conveyance of motor cars to dealers and the docks.

An interesting reference in *Train Illustrated of 1957* remarked on a locomotive working in Australia carrying the builder 's plate inscription, 'Registered British Railways, Western region, no 276, 1948.' It was a Peckett 0-4-0 saddle tank built for the Air Ministry in 1943. For a time it was used at their Cowley depot near Oxford. The Air Ministry sold it to Grays, Middlesex Machinery Merchant in 1950. They in turn sold it to Stewarts & Lloyds (Australia) Ltd and it was at their New South Wales works that it was employed.

Morris Cowley station looking towards Oxford now with a loop in the platform area.

Lens of Sutton

Cold comfort for 6111 tank at Cowley station on January 5, 1963 with the 12.00 pm from Oxford to Princes Risborough.

Laurence Waters

An 'Aberdare' 2-6-0 with a train of cars enclosed in the 'Asmos' vans bound for the Scottish Motor Exhibition in November 1930.

Oxfordshire County Council Photographic Archive

In 1970 the works constructed a bridge over the line to ferry the vehicles over to the new freight terminal using Cartec wagons. This view April 25, 1985.

Brian Higgins

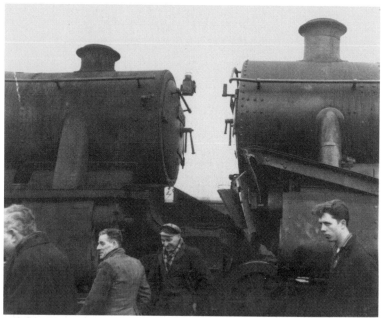

Our Working Lives
Des Perry
Fireman

'I collected the train which was the 12.40 am off Paddington for Banbury. This was a class C perishables. The Loco was 6979 'Helperley Hall'. We went onto the Princes Risborough - Thame - Oxford about 1.00 am. We received the staff for the section from Wheatley to Morris Cowley and set off in all confidence that we had occupation of that section. We were pretty horrified when we looked up ahead, at the car works, and saw an obstruction on the line. We did not dare jump be-

cause in the dark there could be any kind of obstruction alongside the line and many men have been killed doing that. Obviously we applied the brakes then braced ourselves in the cab for the inevitable collision. There were three separated bangs as we hit a fully braked train, it made me think of running straight into a stone wall.'

Des's train had run into 8 Freight no 48134, shunting and preparing a train at the works, having arrived on the Washwood Heath to Morris Cowley freight. Both engines were subsequently repaired and returned to service

Horspath Halt looking towards Oxford on November 11, 1957, 150ft long. In the far distance along the track it is possible to see a little of the car works.

R M Casserley

Horspath Halt

The first Halt here opened on February 1, 1908, with the introduction of the railmotor service, it was just by the underbridge. This was killed off by the war and the subsequent bus services that followed. It closed March 23, 1915 and was pulled down about 1922.

Another Halt was opened at Horspath on June 5, 1933, forty four yards to the west of the former site, this survived until line closure of the passenger service. The Halts for Iffley, Abingdon Road and Hinksey were removed in 1922.

The steep climb to the heights of Shotover came at 1 in 87 to reach a tunnel surveyed at 396 yards. Interestingly this tunnel may well have been joined by another, or replaced, if the plans drawn up by the GWR in 1899 had gone ahead. At the time the Joint Committee of the GWR/GCR had not yet formalised their plans for the line beyond Princes

Risborough. As the GWR were keen to shorten the route to Birmingham they drew up plans to turn this branch into a double track main line by re-aligning and widening the trackbed and putting in place two deviations.

One deviation was at the 53 mp at the road between Gt Milton and Waterstock rejoining the line at Wheatley. The next deviation came just after Wheatley around the existing tunnel with a new huge second tunnel of 907 yards. By 1899 new machinery and techniques ensured that tunnel building was not quite the dread that it had been fifty years earlier. The line then rejoined the old route at the Garsington to Bullingdon Green Road (Roman Way).

In the event the plans for the new line to Aynho Junction with the GCR went ahead as planned and this alternative plan was dropped.

Horspath Halt looking down to the City of Oxford from the train. The chimneys of the car works can be seen in the distance. This view on July 12, 1955.

R M Casserley

Horspath Halt newly replaced in 1933 from the one removed in 1915.
Brunel University, Mowat, Clinker, Wookey Locomotive Collection

One of the original stations on the line at Wheatley close by the village, seen here on April 27, 1957.
To change platforms passengers had to use the road bridge, note the steps alongside.

R M Casserley

Wheatley

A crossing place with a goods yard of two sidings on the 'up'. Speed restriction nearby of 10 mph as train passes over Cooper's Crossing leading to a large timber yard and sawmill close by the line. The signalbox is just beyond this. At Wheatley there is a passing loop, the station is 7 miles 40 chains from Thame. The goods yard had two sidings on the 'up' side. In the Thame direction there was a stone arch bridge over the London Road (A40). With developments and realignment of that road in 1926 this bridge was replaced with one of girder construction.

When it was required to add an extra road to make it dual carriageway in 1962 the bridge was extended with a further girder section, on that occasion the original old stone bridge was demolished. After the line closed the bridge remained for a few years until removal in 1970, when the later section was taken and re-used as a railway bridge in South Wales.

A little further on the River Thame is crossed by another lattice girder type of bridge.

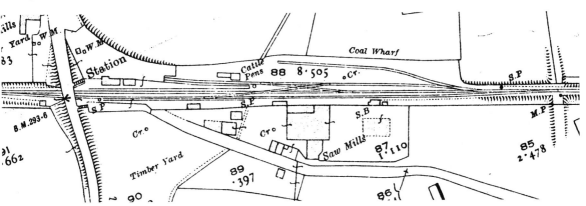

Wheatley station area in 1920, note the road south of the station that originally connected to the station approach across the trackbed area before a bridge was built.

Reproduced by kind permission of Ordnance Survey Crown Copyright NC/01/479

Wheatley seen from the road bridge in 1930, there was a large timber yard close by to the station on the right, a little of its sidings can be seen on the right going into the shed. Note the type of cattle dock alongside the horsebox in the siding.

Brunel University, Mowat, Clinker, Wookey Locomotive Collection

Wheatley seen much later on April 27, 1957. A neat arrangement of buildings albeit in less industrious days.

R M Casserley

A 1400 class on the branch no 1420 on an Oxford to Princes Risborough train at Wheatley on April 27, 1957. The trains on this line in latter years were more commonly the 61XX class

R M Casserley

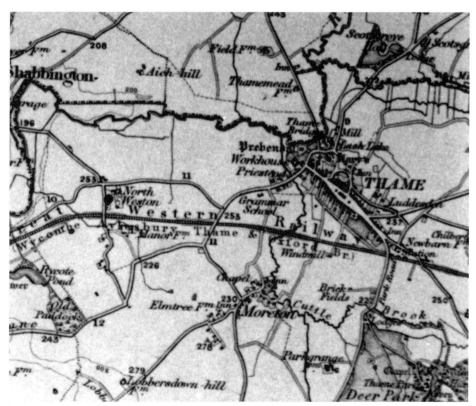

Thame in the 1860's, which was very much the rural market town, the railway close by but not imposing. Thame retains its essential character but is now surrounded by a modern road system.

The station at Tiddington in 1892.

Author's Collection

Tiddington

Tiddington single platform with goods yard of two sidings, coupled with a great deal of milk and goods traffic including Messrs Jarmain's agricultural machinery at Haseley

Tiddington looking towards Oxford on a sunny July 16, 1957. Note the signalbox on the 'down' side and staple traffic, two cattle vans in the siding. Also vegetable garden with beansticks on the left.

R M Casserley

Imposing Brunel style overhead roof at Thame similar to Banbury (Oxfordshire vol 1). The station buildings on the right are of a later style and probably replaced timber. Note how the 'up' side is enclosed within the pediment of the roof but the 'down' side is extended beyond it and supported by columns, see below.

H C Casserley

Thame

The station had a large goods yard with four sidings on the 'up' side. Behind the 'down' platform was a siding with extensive cattle pens built in 1931. The town became noted for its cattle market. It had a population at that time of 2,900.

A feature of the line was that gradient signs on the line were illuminted at night.

An industry that was to benefit so much from the railways was the brick making works. A works existed near Thame near where the A418 road joined Rycote Lane. From 1880 this brick and tile works had a vigorous rail connection to the Oxford - Princes Risborough branch with sidings.

There was a stopping goods daily from Oxford to Thame and back and two trips daily from Oxford to Morris Cowley and back. The new AEC railcars operated between Oxford and Thame in the 1950s and also did a morning run out to Fairford. Oxford had two of these vehicles.

In 1958 an oil terminal with sidings was opened on the Princes Risborough side of the station. This closed down in the mid-nineties. The section between Princes Risborough and Thame has now become a civic amenity with a cycle-, foot- and horsepath.

Thame, detail of the timber roof support of columns.
R M Casserley

Our Working Lives
Ken Bampton
Telegraphist and Signalman

Ken was born in Oxford and lived by the Thame branch where he became a signalman in Cowley Station box. His great friend and mentor was Frank Membury of Wheatley signalbox. In tribute to his friend, Ken wrote the following poem.

A Signalman's Farewell

A Tribute to Francis William Membury, 'Membob' 1899-1989

Call Attention

One beat is line clear please bobbie?
For a very special train
My friend's on his last journey
Away from toil and pain.

Express

Four beats on the bell have sounded
All the signals are showing green
The back boards are off all along the track
As he passes from this scene

On Line

Two beats on the bell are rung now
bring back memories by the score
The glowing grate and the kettle
And his coat hung there by the door.

Signalbox

That polished brown linoleum
Where all mortals fear to tread,
take your shoes off ere you walk it
Or you might end up in bed!

The Frame

Those brightly polished levers
Grab a duster dare you touch
All these things I fond remember
We'll all miss him very much

Train out of section

The train has come and gone now
Two beats plus one have been rung
He has passed from eternal darkness
To the bright everlasting sun.

Rest well dear friend, God bless you.

Ken Bampton, September 1989

The Last Train

A whistle sounds out softly
The guard gives 'right away'
Franks gone down his last branch line,
amongst the flowers and hay.
The crossing gates are open
He passes from our sight
Good night dear friend, God bless you,
Sleep well, sleep long, goodnight

Ken

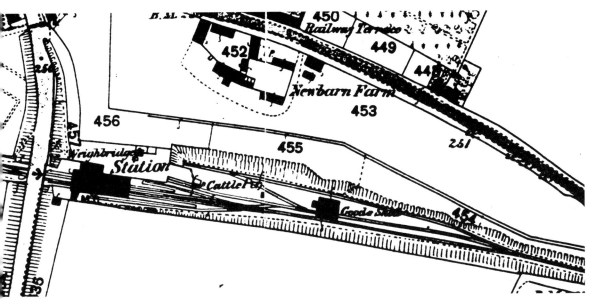

Map of Thame station in 1880, the sidings on the goods shed side were extended ten years or so later.
Reproduced by kind permission of Ordnance Survey Crown Copyright NC/01/479

The bridge between Thame and Wheatley, a second girder span of ninety tons was added on October 21/22 1961. This was part of the development of the London road of the A40 to dual carriageway. Train services on the branch were replaced with buses from Saturday to Monday at 10 am. It was manufactured at the Chepstow works of Fairfields Limited and transported in sections to the site. When doing this the old stone arch of the original railway was discovered in the embankment. When the line closed the new bridge found continuing life in South Wales

Oxford County Council Photographic Collection

Tank engine of the 61XX class no 6138 arrives at Thame from Princes Risborough with a train for Oxford on June 7, 1958.

C R L Coles

A train for Princes Risborough at Thame on May 25, 1962 with no 6129 taking water. The heavy climb out of Oxford took its toll and many engines replenished their water supply at Thame.

R M Casserley

The 6.15 pm Oxford to Princes Risborough train headed by a 61XX 2-6-2 tank engine taking water at Thame on June 6, 1956. Note the distant signalbox and goods shed that closed in 1968.

C R L Coles

LONDON, PRINCES RISBORO', and OXFORD—(Third class only)

Down.

Miles		mrn		mrn	E m	S m		aft	aft E	aft	aft	aft		Sundays mrn		aft	NOTES.
	46 London (Pad.)...dep.	5 40	..	7 40	9 20	9 29		1220	2 ‡ 0	..	4 35	5 23	6 25	..	9 40	..	4 15	
—	Princes Risboro'...dep.	8 10	..	9 47	1122	1122	..	1 52	4 12	..	5 55	6 45	8 0	..	1125	..	5 48	
1½	Bledlow ¶	8 14	..	9 51	1126	1126	..	1 56	4 17	..	5 59	6 50	8 5	..	1131	..	5 52	a Arr 8 8 mrn.
5½	Thame ¶	8 23	..	10 4	1137	1137	..	2 6	4 27	..	6 8	7 15	8 16	..	1144	..	6 3	b Arr 7 36 mrn.
9½	Tiddington............	8 31	..	1013	1144	1144	..	2 14	..	..	7 22	8 24	..	1154	..	6 12	E or£ Except Saturdays
13½	Wheatley ¶	8 42	..	1021	1152	1152	..	2 22	..	..	7 32	8 34	..	12 3	..	6 20	m Limited accommoda-
16½	Morris Cowley........	8 54	..	1031	12 2	1210	..	2 34	..	5 8	7 42	8 48	..	..	..		tion
17½	Littlemore...........	8 58	..	1035	12 6	1214	..	2 35	..	5 13	7 46	8 54	..	1216	..	6 32	S Saturdays only.
21	Oxford 63, 98, 116 arr.	9 10	..	1044	1214	1222	..	2 50	..	5 22	8 5	9 5	..	1228	..	6 40	
84½	103 London (Pad.)..arr.	1055	..	1245	2 25	2 25	..	5 10	..	7 45	..	1110	1145	..	2 35	..	9 35	‡ 5 mins. later on Sats.

Up.

Miles		ngt.		mrn m		mrn		mrn		aft		aft m	aft m	aft	Sundays Sat. ngt.		aft	
—	98 London (Pad.)...dep.	12 0	..	5 30	..	..	..	1120	..	..	..	1 45	..	4 45	12 0	..	4 0	
—	Oxford............dep.	6 55	..	7 30	..	8 18	..	2 38	..	..	..	4 50	..	6 38	7 15	..	5 55	¶ "Halts" at Towersey
3½	Littlemore...........	7 3	..	7 38	..	8 26	..	2 46	..	..	..	4 58	..	6 46	7 23	..	6 3	between Bledlow and
4½	Morris Cowley ¶	7 11	..	7 43	..	8 31	..	2 51	..	..	..	5 2	..	6 52				Thame and at Hors-
7½	Wheatley ¶	7 20	..	7 54	..	8 42	..	3 4	..	..	..	5 13	..	7	27	7 38	..	6 21	path between Wheat-
11½	Tiddington...........	7 27	..	8 0	..	8 50	..	3 10	..	..	..	5 19	..	7 10	7 46	..	6 28	ley and Morris Cowley.
15½	Thame ¶	7645	..	8a52	..	9 10	..	3 20	..	4 45	..	5 27	6 18	7 28	8 1	..	6 39	
19½	Bledlow.......98, 530	7 56	..	9 3	..	9 23	..	3 31	..	4 57	..	5 38	6 30	7 39	8 12	..	6 50	
21	Princes Risboro' 47 arr.	8 0	..	9 8	..	9 27	..	3 38	..	5 2	..	5 43	6 35	7 44	8 16	..	6 54	
55½	47 London (Pad).. arr.	9 34	..	1015	..	1045	..	5 15	..	6 40	..	7 50	9 E 8	9 42	1015	..	8 30	

Timetable for the branch in 1942 from Bradshaw's.

Bill Simpson Collection

Thame in 1930 with 'Metro' tank heading a train of two coaches and cattle wagon. Note cattle trucks, Thame was very much a centre of livestock marketing.

Brunel University / Mowat , Clinker, Wookey Locomotive Collection

View looking east from above, towards Princes Risborough and the signalbox and goods shed.
Brunel University / Mowat , Clinker, Wookey Locomotive Collection

Typical train of the final days of the Thame branch running from Princes Risborough to Oxford, one mile north of Thame with two coaches and a milk wagon. This engine, no 6111, had the melancholy duty of hauling the last passenger train on the Thame branch in January 1963. This view taken on April 24, 1953.

P Waylett

Engine 6149 entering Thame on August 4, 1962 with the 2.52 pm from Oxford to Princes Risborough

H C Casserley

Class 40 no 40122 runs round oil tanks at Thame oil terminal, 1.50 pm September, 1979.

Geoff Gamble

Class 40 no 40127 leaving the oil terminal with empty tankers in April 1979

Geoff Gamble

Towersey Halt looking towards Oxford June 16,1957.

R M Casserley

Towersey Halt

Towersey Halt was opened on June 5, 1933 situated on the 'up' side of an embankment close to the Thame - Towersey - Chinnor Road. Close by was Penn farm Siding that was removed in 1939

A train entering Towersey Halt from Princes Risborough on July 12, 1955.

R M Casserley

One mile east of Thame travelling from Princes Risborough to Oxford, unaccustomed motive power in the shape of 2-10-0 9F 'Evening Star' on a special train in the early Sixties.

Peter Waylett

Bledlow in the summer of 2001

Bill Simpson

Substantially built Bledlow station with a distant train departing to Oxford. Somnolent in sunshine, the country station surrounded with the gentle country sounds and the occasional delicate ring of the block bell heard through the signalbox window. This view on July 23, 1955.

H C Casserley

Bledlow

The single track line to Thame was worked by electric train staff. At just over a mile from the junction at Princes Risborough is Bledlow station, which is about ³/₄ mile from Bledlow Bridge Halt on the Watlington branch.

Bledlow was known for its watercress and elm bowls for trawling nets made by local industry at Longwick. From Bledlow it is four miles from Thame, between is Hinton Crossing that was protected by signals.

View towards Princes Risborough same time as above.

H C Casserley

Princes Risborough with tank engine 6129 under nautical inspection as it prepares to run round the train for the return to Oxford.

Peter E Baughan

The same engine on the same day July 28, 1962 prepares to leave Princes Risborough.

Peter E Baughan

Last days of vintage GWR, the 14XX class no 1426 with motor train set at Princes Risborough on July 26, 1947.
H C Casserley

Princes Risborough

The Wycombe Railway Act of Parliament July 27, 1846 was to build a railway from Maidenhead to High Wycombe. This was opened August 1, 1854 as a broad gauge line, it was leased to the GWR and worked by them.

The Maidenhead station of the time was the one now called Taplow. Under an Act of August 17, 1857 powers were granted to extend the line to Princes Risborough. A later Act of June 28, 1861 gave powers to extend even further to Aylesbury and Oxford.

The section from Wycombe to Thame was opened on August 1, 1862. The line from Princes Risborough to Aylesbury was opened on October 1, 1863. From Thame to Oxford (Kennington Junction) followed on October 24, 1864. In total the WR owned 44 miles 5 chains of broad gauge track. Its existence as an independent company ended on February 1, 1867 when it became part of the GWR.

Upon completion of a working agreement with the Aylesbury & Buckingham Railway (Aylesbury to Verney Junction), the line from Princes Risborough to Aylesbury was narrowed to standard gauge on October 23, 1868.

Two years later the line from Maidenhead to Kennington Junction was converted also.

The pathway from London to Oxford, via Thame to Cheltenham, was much trammelled by high hopes and railway political counterstrokes. In 1836 the London & Birmingham, tried to invade prospective broad gauge territory. This was from Tring on their main line through Aylesbury which was intended to go through Thame.

In 1852 the London & North Western Railway, successors of the L&B, tried to exploit the row between the Oxford, Worcester and Wolverhampton Railway and the GWR and planned a line from Tring to Cheltenham via Thame but were rebuffed by parliament.

Hymek D7026 at Princes Risborough returning from Chinnor cement works on August 10, 1973.

Geoff Gamble

In 1860 the West Midland Railway opposed the Wycombe Railway and proposed a London, Buckinghamshire & West Midland Junction Railway. Further, in 1863, an extension from the East Gloucestershire Railway was proposed. All faltered and the Wycombe line was the only one to serve Thame.

The little over eight mile section from High Wycombe to Princes Risborough became part of the Great Western & Great Central Joint Committee main line. It was then doubled and re-engineered to new alignments to flatten out curves and ease gradients. For a time the station had upper quadrant signals under this management but in April 1962 these reverted back to the standard GWR type.

The main body of the railway eventually became the main line of the amalgam with a new main line route to Birmingham for the GWR and GCR from Northolt Junction to Ashendon Junction, north of Princes Risborough. With pure GWR through to Bicester and Aynho opened on July 1, 1910. The new station began its service with the opening for goods traffic on November 20,

1905 and for passenger trains on April 2, 1906.

The north box at Princes Risborough had ninety working levers.

On January 7, 1963 the passenger service between Oxford and Princes Risborough ceased. In a thick blanket of snow with silver paint on the buffers 2-6-2T no 6111 and in green livery conveyed the last train. In June of the year before, the new 'Western' Diesel hydraulics usurped the former reign of the 'Kings' on the Birmingham expresses through the Chilterns.

The service withered north of Princes Risborough and was single tracked from there to Bicester and Aynho in 1968. During the 1980's a threat of closure was in the air. However with privatisation and the company of Chiltern Railways being formed, trains began running again to a new Birmingham (Snow Hill) station. This required the missing line to be replaced which has been completed between Princes Risborough and Bicester and awaits the same beyond.

Tank engine no 6129 of the 61XX class in the Thame and Watlington bay prepares to leave Princes Risborough on July 28, 1962.

Peter E Baughan

Swirls of activity as 0-6-0 J15 no 65390 leaves Princes Risborough on April 9, 1958 with the Watlington branch goods.

R C Riley

Princes Risborough, as it is very fondly remembered, with an 'up' express thundering through hauled by 5900 'Hinderton Hall', its train including Southern coaches. As it is July 23, 1955 this was no doubt part of the momentum build-up of the holiday season, many passengers heading for the south coast. Hopefully they had chance to enjoy more of the apparent sunshine.

H C Casserley

The 4.32 pm stopping train from Paddington to Bicester hauled by 'Star' 4053 'Princess Alexandra' pauses at Princes Risborough on July 26, 1947. The engine was built in July 1914.

H C Casserley

A class 31 passing the site of Cowley station with a car train in the 1980's photographed from the road bridge used for transporting cars over to the depot. The original depot sidings are on the left.

Laurence Waters

London, High Wycombe, 41a Aylesbury, and Oxford.

LONDON, HIGH WYCOMBE, AYLESBURY, and OXFORD (1st and 3rd class).—Great Western.

Down. — Week Days.

Miles	Down. Paddington Station,	mrn	mrn	mrn	mrn	mrn	mrn	mrn	aft	h	aft	aft	aft	aft	aft	aft	aft	aft	aft	aft	aft		
	London ....dep.	6 55	....	8 10	....	9 30	....	1145	....	1 25	2 40	4 2	....	5 20	....	6 24	7 20	....	....	....	9 0	....	....
1¼	Westbourne Park	6 59	....	....	....	9 33	....	....	....	....	....	....	....	....	....	....	....	....	....	....	....	....	....
5¾	Ealing (Broadway)	....	....	8 21	....	....	....	....	....	....	2c51	....	m	....	....	....	....	....	....	....	9 11	....	....
7¾	Greenford ¶	7 11	....	8 30	....	9 46	....	....	....	1 38	....	4 16	5 9	....	....	6 37	7 32	....	....	....	9 20	....	....
12	Ruislip and Ickenham ..	7 19	....	8 38	....	9 54	....	....	....	1 46	....	4 24	5 19	5 38	....	....	7 40	....	....	....	9 30	....	....
14¾	Denham, for Harefield ..	7 25	....	8 43	....	9 59	....	12 7	....	1 51	3 7	4 29	5 26	5 43	....	6 48	7 45	....	....	....	9 35	....	....
17½	Gerrard's Cross	7 32	....	8 49	....	10 5	Tuesdays only.	1214	....	1 57	3 14	4 35	5 32	5 49	....	6 54	7 51	Saturdays only.	Except Saturdays.	....	9 41	....	....
21½	Beaconsfield	7 40	....	8 58	....	1013		1223	....	2 5	3 22	4 43	Leaves West Ealing at 5 1 aft. Calls at Northolt Junc 5 15 aft.	5 57	....	7 2	7-59			....	9 49	....	....
26½	High Wycombe 44 arr.	7 48	....	9 7	....	1022		1232	....	2 14	3 30	4 52		6 6	....	7 10	8 8			....	9 58	....	....
	High Wycombe dep.	7 50	9 0	9 11	....	1039		1235	....	2 16	3 33	4 55		6 8	....	7 12	8 10			....	10 0	....	....
28¾	West Wycombe	7 55	9 5	9 16	....	1044		1240	....	2 21	3 39	5 0		6 13	....	7 17	8 15			....	10 5	....	....
31½	Saunderton	a	9 11	9 22	....	1049		1245	....	2 26	3 45	5 5		6 18	....	7 23	8 21			....	1010	....	....
34¾	Princes Risboro' 636 arr	8 6	9 17	9 28	....	1055		1251	....	2 32	3 51	5 11		6 24	....	7 29	8 27			m	1016	....	....
—	Princes Risboro' dep.	....	9 20	9 37	....	1056		1258	....	2 33	3 57	5 13		6 26	....	7 33	8 28			9 31	1017	....	....
37½	Little Kimble .. [636	....	....	9 43	....	11 2		1 6	....	2 39	4 3	5 19		6 32	....	7 39	8 34			9 40	1023	....	....
42	Aylesbury † 396, 442	....	9 32	9 52	....	1110		1 15	m	2 47	4 12	5 27		6 40	m	7 47	8 42			9 49	1030	....	....
—	Princes Risboro' ...dep.	8 8	....	9 31	....	....	1110	1254	2 13	....	3 55	....		....	6 33	7 33	....	....	....	....	....	....	....
36¼	Bledlow	8 13	....	9 36	....	....	1115	1 0	2 18	....	4 1	....		....	6 38	7 38	....	m	m	....	....	....	....
40½	Thame	8 24	....	9 46	....	....	1122	1 11	2 30	....	4 12	....		....	7d5	7 47	....	9 5	9 25	....	....	....	....
44½	Tiddington	8 32	....	9 57	m	....	....	1 20	2 41	....	4 23	....		....	7 16	7 55	....	9 16	9 36	....	....	....	....
48	Wheatley ¶	8 45	....	10 6	11 0	....	....	1 28	3b3	....	4 31	....		....	7 26	8 3	....	9 26	9 46	....	....	....	....
52¼	Littlemore ¶ [440, 636	8 54	....	1016	1114	....	....	1 39	3 17	....	4 40	....		....	7 40	8 12	....	9 40	10 0	....	....	....	....
55¾	Oxford 74, 86, 106 arr.	9 1	....	1025	1127	....	....	1 52	3 30	....	4 47	....		....	7 52	8 20	....	9 52	1012	....	....	....	....

Up. — Week Days.

Mls	Up.	mrn	mrn	mrn	m	mrn	mrn	mrn	m	mrn	m	aft	aft	aft	aft	aft	m	aft	aft	aft	m	m	aft
—	Oxford ¶ ....dep.	....	....	....	Arrives West Ealing 9 22 mrn. Calls at Northolt Junc. 9 8 mrn.	7 45	8 23	....	1025	1120	1 2	....	2 28	Saturdays only.	....	....	4 40	....	6 20	....	8 15	8 35	....
3½	Littlemore ¶	....	....	....		7 55	8 32	....	1038	1129	1 14	....	2 40		....	....	4 54	....	6 30	....	8 28	8 48	....
7¼	Wheatley	....	....	....		8 5	8 43	....	1051	1139	1 29	....	2 50		....	....	5 8	....	6 42	....	8 42	9 2	....
11¼	Tiddington	....	....	....		8 15	8 54	....	....	1146	1 38	....	2 57		....	....	5 17	....	6 54	....	8 51	9 11	....
15¼	Thame	....	....	....		8 25	9 8	....	....	1157	1 49	....	3 7		4 30	....	5n33	....	7 6	....	9 1	9 21	....
19½	Bledlow	....	....	....		8 34	9 19	....	....	12 7	2 0	....	3 16		4 40	....	5 45	....	7 17	....	....	....	....
21	Princes Risboro' 636 arr	....	....	....		8 39	9 24	....	....	1212	2 5	....	3 21		4 48	....	5 50	....	7 22	m	....	....	....
—	— Aylesbury (Joint) dep	7 10	7 50	8 15		....	9 5	1010	....	1150	....	1 55	3 5	3 20	Tuesdays only.	4 50	....	5 50	7 9	9 5	....	....	....
—	4½ Little Kimble	7 18	7 59	8 23		....	9 13	1018	....	12 2	....	2 3	3 13	3 28		4 58	....	5 58	7 17	9 15	....	....	....
—	7¼ Princes Risboro' 636	7 24	8 5	8 29		....	9 19	1024	....	1210	....	2 9	3 19	3 34		5 6	....	6 4	7 23	9 22	....	....	....
—	Princes Risboro' ....dep.	7 25	8 7	8 30		8 41	9 29	1025	....	1214	....	2 13	3 25	3 36		5 9	....	6 5	7 31	Stop	Saturdays only.	Except Saturdays.	9 26
24¼	Saunderton	7 32	8 14	....		8 49	9 36	1032	....	1221	....	2 20	3 32	3 45		5 16	....	6 12	7 39				9 33
27	West Wycombe	7 37	8 19	....		8 54	9 41	1037	....	1226	....	2 25	3 37	3 52		5 21	....	6 17	7 46	....			9 39
29¼	High Wycombe 44 arr.	7 42	8 23	8 43		8 59	9 46	1042	....	1231	....	2 30	3 42	3 58		5 25	....	6 22	7 51	aft			9 45
	High Wycombe dep.	7 45	8 30	....		9 1	9 49	1044	....	1234	....	2 35	3 44	4 2		5 35	....	6 24	7 55	8 0			10 5
34¼	Beaconsfield	7 55	8 39	....		9 10	9 58	1054	....	1244	....	2 45	3 53	4 11		5 45	....	6 33	....	8 10			1015
38¼	Gerrard's Cross	8 4	8 47	....	8 52	9 18	10 6	11 3	....	1253	....	2 54	4 1	4 20		5 54	....	6 42	....	8 19			1024
41	Denham, for Harefield ..	8 9	8 52	....	8 58	9 24	1011	11 8	....	....	....	2 59	4 6	4 25	....	5 59	....	6 47	....	8 24			1029
43¾	Ruislip and Ickenham ¶	8 14	8 57	....	9 4	9 30	1017	1113	....	....	....	3 4	4 11	4 30	....	6 4	....	6 52	....	8 29			1034
48	Greenford	8 22	....	....	9 15	....	....	....	....	1 7	....	3 12	....	n	....	6 12	....	7 0	....	8 37			....
51½	Ealing (Broadway)	....	....	....	....	....	....	1126	....	....	....	....	....	....	....	....	....	7 7	9 13	8 46			1047
54½	Westbourne Park	....	....	....	....	....	....	....	....	....	....	....	....	....	....	....	....	....	9 26	....			1058
55¾	London (Paddingtn) arr.	8 35	9 15	....	....	9 48	1035	1139	....	1 20	....	3 25	4 30	....	....	6 27	....	7 20	9 30	8 59			11 2

Down. — Sundays.

Paddington Station,	mrn	mrn (Calls at West Ealing at 11 24 mrn. and Northolt Junction at 11 39 mrn.)	m (Calls at Acton 12 55 and West Ealing at 1 3 aft.)	aft (Calls at Northolt Junction at 2 39 aft.)	aft	aft	
London ....dep.	9 23	1110	1245	2 15	5 0	8 55	....
Westbourne Park	....	....	1249	....	5 4	9 0	....
Ealing (Broadway)	9 34	1121	1 0	2 26	5 13	9 10	....
Greenford ¶	9 43	1130	1 11	2 35	5 22	9 19	....
Ruislip and Ickenham ..	9 52	1140	1 23	2 44	5 30	9 27	....
Denham, for Harefield ..	9 57	1145	1 30	2 49	5 35	9 32	....
Gerrard's Cross	10 3	1150	1 36	2 55	5 41	9 38	....
Beaconsfield	1011	1158	1 44	3 3	5 49	9 46	....
High Wycombe 44 arr.	1020	12 7	1 54	3 12	5 58	9 55	....
High Wycombe dep.	1022	....			....	9 57	....
West Wycombe	1027	....			....	10 3	....
Saunderton	1032	....			....	10 9	....
Princes Risboro' 640 arr.	1038	....			....	1015	....
Princes Risboro' ..dep.	1043	....			....	1018	....
Little Kimble ... [640	1049	....			....	....	....
Aylesbury † 396, 442,	1056	....			....	1030	....
Princes Risboro' ....dep.	1041	....			....	1017	....
Bledlow	1046	....			....	1023	....
Thame	1059	....			....	1032	....
Tiddington	1112	....			....	1041	....
Wheatley ¶	1122	....			....	1051	....
Littlemore ¶ [440, 640	1130	....			....	11 1	....
Oxford 78, 88, 106, arr.	1138	....			....	11 8	....

Up. — Sundays.

Up.	mrn	mrn	aft	aft (Calls at Northolt Junction at 2 48 aft.)	aft (Calls at West Ealing at 6 2 aft.)	aft	aft		
Oxford ¶ ....dep.	6 40	....	....			5 55	....	....	....
Littlemore ¶	6 50	....	....			6 5	....	....	....
Wheatley	7 3	....	....			6 16	....	....	....
Tiddington	7 17	....	....			6 24	....	....	....
Thame	7 35	....	....			6 34	....	....	....
Bledlow	7 45	....	....			6 44	....	....	....
Princes Risboro' 640 arr.	7 50	....	....			6 49	....	....	....
Aylesbury (Joint) dep.	7 30	....	....			6 32	....	....	....
Little Kimble	7 40	....	....			6 42	....	....	....
Princes Risboro' 640	7 46	....	....			6 48	....	....	....
Princes Risboro' ....dep.	7 53	....	....			6 53	....	....	....
Saunderton	8 0	....	....			7 0	....	....	....
West Wycombe	8 6	....	....			7 6	....	....	....
High Wycombe 44 arr.	8 11	....	m			7 11	....	....	....
High Wycombe dep.	8 14	1030	2 0	2 15	5 15	7 15	9 55	....	....
Beaconsfield	Via Maidenhead.	1040	2 11	2 25	5 25	7 25	10 5	....	....
Gerrard's Cross		1049	2 20	2 34	5 34	7 34	1014	....	....
Denham, for Harefield ..		1054	2 25	2 39	5 39	7 39	1019	....	....
Ruislip and Ickenhem ¶		1059	....	2 44	5 44	7 44	1024	....	....
Greenford		11 8	....	2 53	5 53	7 53	1033	....	....
Ealing (Broadway)	9 41	1117	....	3 2	6 5	8 2	1042	....	....
Westbourne Park	9 55	1127	....	3 12	6 16	8 13	1052	....	....
London (Paddington) arr.	10 0	1130	....	3 15	6 20	8 17	1055	....	....

a Stops to set down from London on informing Guard at Paddington. b Arrives at 2 49 aft. c Stops to take up.
d Arrives at 6 48 aft. h Calls at Perivale Halt on Saturdays to set down on informing Guard at Paddington.
n Arrives at 5 27 aft. m Motor Car, one class only. n Arrives Northolt Jn. 4 34 aft. † Nearly a mile to L. & N. W. Station.
¶ "Halts" at Northolt, between Greenford and Ruislip and Ickenham; Horsepath and Garsington Bridge, between Wheatley and Littlemore; and Iffley, Abingdon Road, and Hinksey, between Littlemore and Oxford.

. For Motor Cars between Paddington, Westbourne Park, and Denham, see page 41b.

Bradshaws Railway Guide for 1909.

Author's Collection

The Watlington branch train at Princes Risborough on July 23, 1955.

H C Casserley

Princes Risborough as it looked in the mid-eighties when the GWR/GCR footbridge to the 'down' platform for Thame and Watlington branches was still in situ, though rustily unused. On the left is the bay for the Aylesbury trains.

Bill Simpson

The Thame branch was noted for the use of AEC diesel railcars, here no 11 in its GWR livery at Swindon in the 1950's.

Laurence Waters

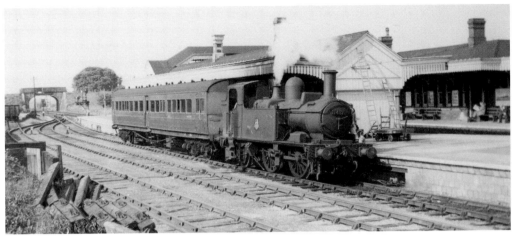

The Abingdon branch train at Radley on May 28, 1957 with engine no 1437.

R M Casserley

CHAPTER 4

ABINGDON

The welcome of the railway to Abingdon seems somewhat chequered, the GWR in supporting the Oxford Railway included a branch to Abingdon in the Bill of 1837. As described in the early history this was a triumph for those opposing the railway as it failed by influence of the House of Lords. The branch was included in later submissions in 1838 but was opposed again, by the Abingdon Member of Parliament, a Mr Duffield, MP. Some of the townspeople have claimed that the town did in fact want a railway which seems odd in respect of the MP supposedly representing the views of his constituents.

The successful promotion of the Oxford Railway in 1842 deleted the branch altogether, like the situation of Steventon, the GWR would allow forces of persuasion to take their course. The station of Abingdon Road, later named Culham, serving the town. Other schemes included Abingdon in their proposals, particularly a new line to Chel-

tenham by the GWR which was another ploy in the conflict between them and their competitor the LNWR. When the LNWR were defeated the GWR also withdrew their expensive notion of this new line.

In 1855 the people of Abingdon promoted the Abingdon Railway with a scheme for a branch from the main line near Radley of two miles, with a ruling gradient of 1 in 200. This was authorised in June of that year. The Abingdon Railway bought land from the Corporation in Stert Street for £472 pounds. The line was a modest undertaking with very little in the way of earthworks and costing £25,000. As the county town of Berkshire in the nineteenth century it seems unthinkable that Abingdon should not have a railway and in view of main line schemes a branch seems a diminished compromise. Probably the reason why this role passed to Reading.

On June 2, 1856 the line opened with wooden platforms on the main line to provide a junction station called Abingdon Junction. The station of Radley did not open until 1873. The line was opened in the broad gauge with the GWR leasing the locos and stock to run eight trains each way daily. The occasion was marked with a customary champagne dinner in celebration in the Guild Hall attended by G D Gooch. At a more basic level 120 navvies were treated to a celebration at the 'Rising Sun' public house.

An immediate benefit from the arrival of the railway was the drop in coal price from 25 shillings a ton to 16 shillings which, to communities of the period so dependent on this fuel cannot be over emphasised. The town used 30,000 tons per annum.

The people of Abingdon hoped to gain from the resistance of Oxford University to allow the GWR to build a carriage works in Oxford in 1865. They prevailed upon the GWR to come to the town to the extent of suggesting using land by Nuneham railway bridge and Baron Court Farm, a third of a mile east of the station. They offered the railway a loan of £20,000 and to give half of the land required. But the GWR were worried about flooding which does seem a little odd as this was not exactly an unknown problem around the Oxford station area which had been flooded many times However it would appear that the serious alternative was Swindon where the works were finally built

On November 26,1872 the line was converted to narrow gauge to coincide with the opening of the new station at Radley the following year. The branch runs for three quarters of a mile alongside the main line before turning sharply towards the town.

The new railway, it seems, was not entirely satisfactory to local needs as a deputation from the Abingdon Railway went to Paddington to see if improvements could be made to the local service, in 1891. The local company did in fact enjoy forty per cent of receipts for gross traffic until the undertaking was finally absorbed by the GWR in 1904.

The company could not have invested much into the facilities as these were much complained of and, when in 1908 as a result of a shunting mishap the roof was badly damaged, some rebuilding had to be undertaken. To the credit of the GWR the result was a very attractive station building block at the end of the terminus and a new substantial roof, less attractive, covered in corrugated iron.

The branch ran its trains on the train ticket system when passenger and freight trains worked the line. A journey time was little more than five minutes. The train ran sixteen return trips daily during the week and ran three trips on Sunday.

A leather industry was established in Abingdon from early years reaching a peak in the period of the 1914-18 war. The Pavlova Leather Company increased production for military coats, boots, belts, harnesses, etc, for the war. They enlarged their premises to cope with the new demand but with the end of the war it became redundant space and by 1929 the area of the factory alongside Marchant Road was largely unused. This area appealed to a man called Cecil Kimber who could see the potential of these premises and the building was leased by Morris Garages for assembly of their MG cars. Production was transferred from Edmund's Road, Oxford to Abingdon in 1930 and a motoring legend was born. It proved to be a very useful move for the railway. The branch line brought in materials and loaded the finished product to carry that famous badge to all corners of the world; the famous sports car emanating from a single branch line station!

In 1953 the Locomotive steam shed was closed and operations became much scaled down when afternoon workings ceased. Trains were now rostered from Oxford. In 1954 the levers and signals were removed from the signalbox and the points leading from the running line to the yard, and the run-round loop, were worked from a two-lever ground frame, released by a key. The line was then worked on a one-engine-in-steam system which simplified running to the most basic. In 1956 the signalbox was utilised as a workers' canteen. The gasworks siding ceased to be used in 1956.

It was worked in the early days by broad gauge tank engines when they became eastablished from the tender engines. Later '517', 'Metro' tanks and pannier tanks took their turns, but few 0-6-0 engines were seen after 1954. It will be mostly remembered for the 0-4-2T '14XX' class on push-pull with the

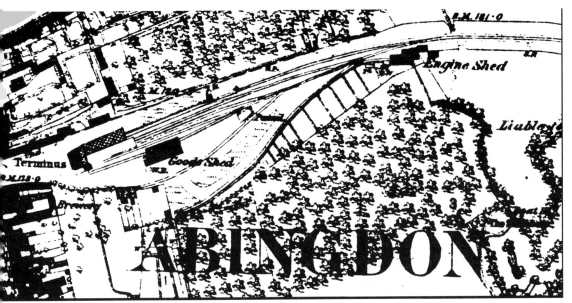

Abingdon station layout in 1875, note the engine shed well beyond the station and the long siding from that point to the outer edge of the goods yard.

Reproduced by kind permission of Ordnance Survey Crown Copyright NC/01/479

engine at the Abingdon end of a single 'Motor' coach and christened 'The Abingdon Bunk'. The coach was kept overnight at Radley except on Saturdays when it was taken to Oxford for cleaning. The engine returned each night to Oxford shed then came back to Radley at 6.15 am. It would pick up the coach and run an early morning parcels train to Abingdon.

The passenger service began with the 7.5 am train from Abingdon which continued to work the morning trains until the 11.55 am from Radley. After working the evening service it would then return light engine to Oxford. On Saturdays it worked the coach through to Oxford and returned with it for the Sunday evening workings. Freight services and one mid-day passenger return trip were worked by one of the Oxford 0-6-0 pannier tanks '850' class. The loco worked the 10.50 freight for Hinksey Yard and then waited for fifty-five minutes at Radley for traffic off the Didcot - Oxford freight. The train continued on to reach Abingdon at 12.35 pm. In the absence of the regular loco the freight engine worked one passenger train, leaving Abingdon at 1.15 pm. It returned from Radley at 1.40 pm having run-round there as the train was not push-pull fitted.

The passenger service was poorly patronised and was easily competed against by the local bus service to Oxford and ceased on September 8, 1963.

The branch goods traffic was no modest assemblage of local assortments but very substantial with coal, beer, barley, beet and pelts for the Pavlova Tannery which sent down the steam lorries to collect them from the yard. Cattle were driven through the streets to and from the station from the weekly market, also polo ponies which were trained and transported from Abingdon.

The opening of the Royal Air Force aerodrome in September 1932, RAF Abingdon, increased the traffic flow further.

Even the daily goods train from Hinksey at 10.30 am was handled by the '1400' class that shunted the yard in the afternoon and went back to Hinksey at 4.35 pm. The line continued from steam to diesel with type 2 diesel hydraulics working the the prodigious daily goods traffic demands, essentially with the MG cars which continued until 1980 when the car works closed.

For the Abingdon Festival of May 25, 1970 the GWR Society held an exhibition in the terminus.

Abingdon station in 1933, note the substantial train of cattle wagons.
Brunel University / Mowat , Clinker, Wookey Locomotive Collection

Our Working Lives
Bill Simpson
Author

'I had the good fortune to have the opportunity to travel the branch on a special 'last train' operating day in 1984 when three dmu trains shuttled from Oxford to Abingdon by

British Rail. It was a warm sunny day made more poignant by the brilliance of thousands of bright red poppies on subsoil near the junction, contrasting with the fullness of the green countryside. Time worn, but effective as a historical totem, was the fixed distant signal, shortly before the station.

Crowds circulated the station, enjoyed the sunshine and looked at the few buildings that remained; the stables for instance. An interesting comparison could be made with the first station that was impressively painted with a broad gauge engine on the public house sign close by. It was a memorable day of crowded trains with good humoured people Many reflecting on their memories of the line and how often they had used it in the course of their daily travels. The station area is now built over and the Abingdon Railway is a part of the history of the town, a fond memory of the little train that served it so well for over a hundred years.

One of the 94XX class 0-6-0PT no 9421 a Hawksworth design introduced in 1947. Seen here entering Radley on May 28, 1957 with a train of mineral wagons. The Abingdon branch line is on the right.

R M Casserley

Abingdon from beyond the platform in 1933, beyond the train of wagons facing the locomotive shed is an open cab pannier tank.

Brunel University: Mowat , Clinker, Wookey Locomotive Collection,

Local private owner coal wagon held at Didcot GWS

Bill Simpson

At the station no 5816 on May 28, 1957

R M Casserley

Abingdon locomotive shed and coaling stage with gas lamp. This perfect small space saving arrangement is often depicted on model railways of GWR termini. Note also the raised coach body on the area opposite and the dominating water tank. This photograph taken on May 14, 1951.

R C Riley

Detail at Abingdon, left to right, goods office once alongside goods shed, now demolished, stables and office/store.

Geoff Gamble

The main platform in the fifties, note the car loading vehicles on the siding to the right. Also the cars of the period, particularly the Morris.

RAS Marketing

Abingdon in the diesel age, a single unit with 'chevron' or 'cats whisker' livery. This working ran to Oxford station.

Laurence Waters

Abingdon station front in 1958. An impressively robust looking building compared to its predecessor, looking like a small bank.

B W Leslie

Two-coach dmu entering Abingdon in the early Sixties, Abingdon having just moved into the diesel period before closure in 1963. The obviously well stocked goods sidings continued on for much longer.

Laurence Waters

After closure of the station to passengers it retained a vigorous service in goods work. There was a lot of coal but the most outstanding feature was the shipment of the famous MG cars from the nearby works. The following are a number of photographs supplied by Les Burley showing the cars being loaded in 1980.

Les Burley

The casual wear of the man instructing the driver on loading, contrasts with the safety wear insisted upon today.

Les Burley

A view looking from the buffer end with the maltsters building on the left distance, now demolished, and the goods shed on the right.

Les Burley

The end loading ramp called for some careful handling by the drivers of these brand new cars.

Les Burley

The pride of Abingdon and Britain assembled on the platform.

Les Burley

An imaginative angle on things from the inside the goods shed, note recently removed track leading into the shed.

Les Burley

The maltsters building provides a background to the progressive line of cars.

Les Burley

A view from the platform end of an Abingdon site now gone forever beneath a supermarket.

Les Burley

A class 31 no 31121 departs with the shipment from Abingdon

Les Burley

The 'Last Day of Service' day on the Abingdon branch in 1984. Crowds enjoyed fine weather to reflect a little, and a ceremony to say goodbye.

Bill Simpson

British Rail

Abingdon Branch Line
LAST DAY of SERVICE
30th June 1984

Oxford
Radley
Abingdon

valid for one return journey from Oxford to Abingdon on date shown. Available on 11.05/13.05 train only

306

Souvenir Ticket £3.00

Issued subject to British Railways Board conditions of carriage

The public house sign alongside the station based on a photograph of broad gauge days.

Bill Simpson

The stables converted to more modern transport requirements.

Geoff Gamble

The original station at Abingdon, therefore prior to rebuilding in 1909. The train of distinctive length is headed by the familiar 'Metro' 2-4-0 tank engine.

Laurence Waters Collection

A regular '517' class 522 in front of the gasworks. Though humble in duty the engine is neverthless highly polished. A matter of some personal pride to the men that worked with her and would be proud of her minor role alongside any main line engine pausing at Radley.

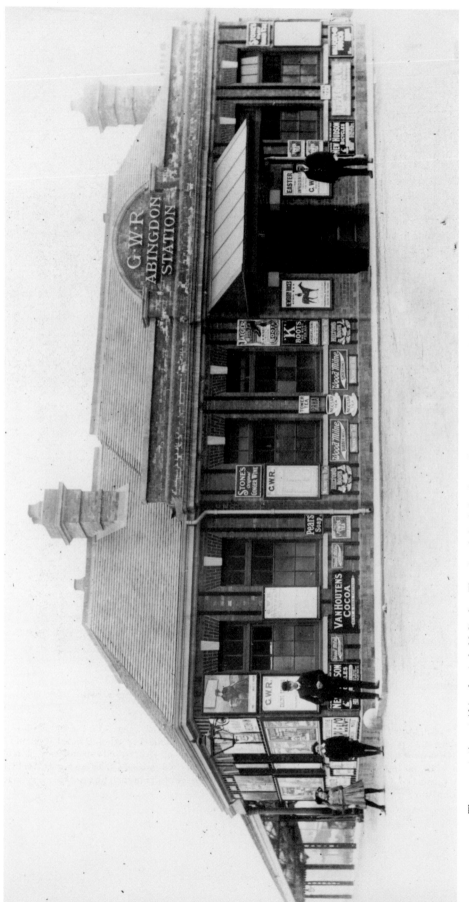

The new station at Abingdon in bold display. The sign, left of the door advertises trains to Newbury Races in April, with a station on the course. Whilst the sign on the right advertises Easter trains on the GWR in 1910. And what would any self respecting station be without a sign for Mazawattee Tea or Van Houtens Cocoa?

Laurence Waters Collection

A '517' 0-4-2 tank and train arriving from Radley with auto coach. Behind is the malthouse and further distant the gasworks. Obviously the rebuilt station is in place so this has to be post 1909 and probably post First World War. The '517' class was displaced for scrapping by the 14XX class.

Laurence Waters Collection

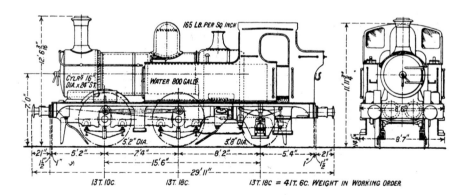

The little gem, the '1400' class that was a modernised version of an older class as far back as 1868. These older engines were replaced with 95 new engines numbered 4800-74 push-pull fitted and nos 5800-19 that were not. The new engines had extended smokebox and modernised cab and were all built between 1932 and 1936. Numbers 4800-74 were renumbered in 1946 to 1400-74. These handsome little engines with a GWR auto coach became the quintessential image of the branch line railway, very much so in Oxfordshire.

A selection of photographs taken in 1985 before demolition, not to emphasise decline, but as a
final record of how the station looked as it awaited its inevitable fate of disappearing under a
supermarket.

Bill Simpson

The main platform end.

Bill Simpson

Ground frame controlling the sidings from the main platform, this replaced the signalbox control.
Bill Simpson

The line trailing off among the trees to Radley and for many years, the link to the world beyond.
Bill Simpson

The GWR were great advocates of the 0-6-0 tank engine and would have a thousand in service at any one time. No 2036 is obviously in the vintage livery of its builders as it stands before the gasworks at Abingdon. As alway proudly polished.

A respite on April 9, 1927 as branch tank engine 1498 takes time at Oxford, possibly for a boiler wash out.

H C Casserley

In the splendid Town Hall designed by Christopher Wren the good men of the Corporation of Abingdon met and worked towards the goal of placing their town on the railway map. Though never on the main line that they would have liked the railway did at last arrive and served the town for one hundred and twenty years.

Bill Simpson

N Stead

Remote, beneath the Chiltern Hills, the small town station of Watlington. That the transport needs of a town could be served in this way seems so very far removed from our modern, times and our almost contemptuous regard for distance. It may seem archaic and incovenient now but few would not view this and the following photographs without some sense of loss.

No 1426 of the '1400' class at Princes Risborough on July 26, 1947. An ideal combination of push-pull for working the branch with quick acceleration from any stops in a short distance.

H C Casserley

CHAPTER 5

WATLINGTON BRANCH

Princes Risborough is, of course in Buckinghamshire but forms a conclusion to the end of the Thame branch from Oxford, it also operates as the beginning of the line to Watlington which runs back into Oxfordshire.

The first attempt for the railway to reach Watlington was a Wallingford & Watlington Railway Act of July 27, 1864. The railway would take a route south of the Thames and would connect Watlington with the GWR main line at Cholsey & Moulsford (Wallingford Road), in the event, only the line as far as Wallingford was built, this opened on February 7, 1866.

The next attempt was for a light railway by a private Company supported by the Earl of Macclesfield, this was the Act for the Watlington & Princes Risborough Railway which received the Royal Assent on July 26, 1869. The Earl of Macclesfield's home was near the subsequent terminus and was called Shirburn Castle.

The line of 8 miles, 66 chains was opened on August 15, 1872 with three trains each way daily on weekdays. It gave an undertaking that the line would be worked on the ticket system but it was in fact worked on the one engine in steam system. Later it was worked by electric train staff incorporating a key for unlocking the points. It was worked also by auto train although run-round facilities existed at each end. This was on a speed restriction of 30 mph.

Stock to run the line was hired from the GWR. A connection was made at Princes Risborough with the GWR for goods traffic, but passengers had to use two short wooden platforms and station buildings at a crossing place that was built beyond the main station.

Capital for the line was established at

£36,000 with borrowing powers for a further £12,000.

In 1876 the Company owed £2,000 to the GWR with little prospect of settling the debt so they were permitted to repay at 3% interest. Consequently a new agreement came about to rent access to the GWR station at Princes Risborough for five years at a cost of £250 per annum. This agreement would not be concluded until December 31, 1881.

The local company worked the line for the first eleven years until it was absorbed by the GWR who acquired powers from July 1, 1883. A virtual rescue from a shakey financial situation. There was some rancour amongst shareholders that all would be handed over to the GWR and some bitterness that the GWR would not acquiesce to completing the line to Wallingford, Didcot or Oxford. Also that it would be virtually handed over without any investors seeing any kind of return on their investment.

The first Manager was J G Rowe who also managed the Aylesbury & Buckingham Railway, a no less shaky company. He also exerted influence over its own little branch of the Duke of Buckingham's to Brill.

The Watlington Railway had tried to find agreement with the GWR to run the line at a rental from them of £600 pa, this the GWR refused owing to the primitive nature of the construction.

As it was the the GWR had to bear the cost of modifying some of the engineering work to ease the gradients. Actual possession of the line was not completed until December 31, 1883. The GWR then needed to authorise expenditure of £3,750 to do necessary works on the line as it had been built following closely to the contours of the land on chalk ballast to economise on engineering works. The stations between at the opening were Chinnor and Aston Rowant.

The GWR reasoned that the line would be ideal for the railmotor vehicle system that had been developed over all the the country's railways up until the First World War. They therefore introduced a service on the branch in 1906. This introduced a number of rail level halts at Bledlow Bridge (1 mile 52 chains), Kingston Crossing (5 miles 17 chains), protected by working distant signals, the only working signals on the branch.

Lewknor Bridge (7 miles 4 chains), another, Wainhill Halt (2 miles 75 chains), was opened in 1925.

A journey on the branch in 1872 was some thirty minutes duration. The locomotive used being a Sharp Stewart, a 2-2-2WT with driving wheels of 5ft 6in, this was number 1, it was scrapped in 1883. Another Sharp Stewart 2-4-0 side tank with driving wheels of 4ft then worked the line. This was originally numbered by the GWR 1384 but became number 2 on the branch. It was rebuilt by the GWR at Swindon in 1899, but finally ended its days on the Colonel Steven's line of the West Cleverdon & Portishead Railway in 1937 after being sold to that railway by the GWR IN 1903.

In terms of the twentieth century the line was commonly associated with the ubiquitous GWR 57XX pannier tank engine running five trains each way daily. With the closure of the engine shed at Watlington in 1956 the engine for the branch was supplied by Slough shed (81B). To reach the branch the engine left Slough at 5.38 am and arrived at Watlington at 7 am. In the evening it left Watlington at 9 pm and arrived back at Slough at 10.50 pm. Occasionally a 0-4-2T 14XX was seen on the line. In February 1955 a J68 0-6-0 tank from Aylesbury shed was tried on the line but its water capacity was found to be insufficient. Another engine to work the line in 1958 was an 0-6-0 tender engine no 65390, the only recorded occasion of a tender engine on the branch.

On June 29, 1957 the last 'Watlington Flyer' ran with engine no 4650 hauling a full train as the rites of closure were presided over by local dignatories. The line officially closed July 1, its service was replaced by City of Oxford Motor Services.

Freight services between Chinnor and Watlington were withdrawn January 2, 1961, the last goods train to Watlington being run on Friday, December 30, 1960. This was hauled by 2-6-2T 41272 of Bedford shed. The track from Chinnor onwards was lifted early in 1963. The track along the branch was cut up in 20ft lengths and stacked in the yard at Aston Rowant from where it was hauled away by the contractors diesel locomotive early in 1963.

Coal stage at Watlington on July 18, 1967

Geoff Gamble

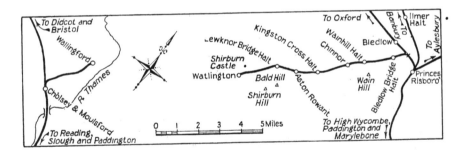

The two railways apart and a historical might have been had a connection between the two been realised. Although, apart from local interests, this would appear a dubious advantage to the railway system.

Railway Magazine

WATLINGTON AND PRINCES RISBOROUGH RAILWAY.

LEAVE.	WEEK DAYS ONLY.							LEAVE.	WEEK DAYS ONLY.						
	A.M.	A.M.	A.M.	P.M.	P.M.	P.M.	P.M.		A.M.	A.M.	A.M.	P.M.	P.M.	P.M.	P.M.
Watlington	...	9 5	...	2 25	...	5 45	...	Risborough	...	1030	...	3 40	...	6 35	...
Aston Rowant	...	9 13	...	2 33	...	5 56	...	Chinnor	...	1043	...	3 50	...	6 45	...
Chinnor	...	9 20	...	2 40	...	6 7	...	Aston Rowant	...	1054	...	3 57	...	6 52	...
Risborough	...	9 30	...	2 50	...	6 20	...	Watlington	...	11 5	...	4 5	...	7 0	...

Timetable for the Watlington and Princes Risborough Railway in 1894, not exactly a bustle of activity. By this time the Company was in the hands of the GWR

Bill Simpson Collection

Princes Risborough a railway junction destined to greater things from its inception of the early days of the GWR when it was a station on the Wycombe Railway. Seen here on April 9, 1958, with interestingly, J15 no 65390 on the Watlington branch train whilst the tank engine of the former GWR leaves with a single coach for the Thame branch to Oxford.

R C Riley

Princes Risborough

Opened as an intermediate station on the Wycombe Railway to Thame on August 1, 1862 the station was in a crucial position for development. Trains came up through the gap of the Chilterns to reach the open lands enclosing the Vale of Aylesbury and prospects beyond. This position was taken advantage of dramatically, at first with a branch to Aylesbury in 1863. Later the Watlington branch was built in the standard gauge from a junction with the Thame line in 1872.

Railway politics at the turn of the century saw an alliance between the newly formed Great Central Railway that had forged its new extension to London over the fractious concession of the Metropolitan Railway to their own terminus at Marylebone.

The GWR were incensed that they could not compete with their old rivals the LNWR on their west coast route with two hour ex-presses to Birmingham from London on their line via Didcot and Oxford. The two railways then established a Joint Committee to administer an alliance between them to build a four track railway advantaging both their lines, the GCR from Northolt to Ashendon Junction, the GWR further to Aynho and to join their old route via Oxford, this was completed in 1910.

The upshot of this was that Princes Risborough was completely rebuilt in 1906, as it appears in the Thame chapter.

Although the Birmingham line runs very successfully as Chiltern Railways route, with new building at Princes Risborough on the 'down' side. The branches to Thame and Watlington are now consigned to memory, apart from the Chinnor and Princes Risborough Railway, and photographs like those in the following pages.

Bledlow Bridge Halt on July 27, 1955 looking towards Princes Risborough.
H C Casserley

Bledlow Bridge Halt

In 1906 a steam railcar service was introduced on the branch to improve the passenger receipts. To operate this service a number of Halts were opened, Bledlow Bridge being one of them. They were built with only the most essential requirement, low level platforms, as steps were attached to the railmotor coach for boarding. A name board and oil lamps with a small wood shelter were all that they had. However this Halt was closer to Bledlow than the station on the Thame line called Bledlow.

The Halt looking towards Watlington with a distant train, hauled by a pannier tank, on July 23, 1955
H C Casserley

A Princes Risborough train leaving Wainhill Crossing Halt on May 21, 1956 hauled by former GWR pannier tank
C R L Coles

Wainhill Crossing Halt on June 12, 1957 and crossing keeper's house

R M Casserley

In later years of the workings just to the cement works the train crews operated the gates themselves. Here driver of 31136 climbs down to do this as the train returns with empties on February 15, 1978.

Geoff Gamble

Chinnor station and distant cement works on September 13, 1958

H C Casserley

Man and scythe at Chinnor station on June 12, 1957

R M Casserley

Chinnor station small and attractive, in the local building style of flint, brick and stone. Demolished, then restored to life by the good work of the Chinnor and Princes Risborough Railway and very much worth a visit. This view on September 23, 1951.

R C Riley

Chinnor

The first station from Princes Risborough on the branch showing the first of the two intermediate stations with the building pattern of the Watlington Railway station buildings. It is situated three miles and fifty-seven chains from Princes Risborough. It is a variation of the twin gable design, enclosing the entrance porch similar to a style used by the LNWR at Brackley, Buckingham, Winslow and Bicester. On this branch they are oranmantal, like small chapels. Beyond the station on the 'up' side was the goods yard with two sidings.

Some improvements were made to goods facilities at Chinnor in 1911. Lime producing began in the area of the station late in the nineteenth century using bottle kilns;

these were replaced in 1920. The works opened for cement production in 1928 and sidings were run from the station to it. Coal was brought in from East Midland collieries and gypsum from Kegworth in Nottinghamshire. Whilst empty cement wagons returned from Parkstone near Poole in Dorset.

Deliveries were 400 wagons of coal each month, 1,300 tons of gypsum. Although both these commodities increased over the years, as essential raw materials, the output from the works gradually went by road. From 1908 to 1919 production went out by rail, including cement, up until 1928. Gradually this was reduced until the amount by rail became negiligble; road development and larger lorries were a powerful inducement away from

Chinnor as it appeared in the 1930's, note the sidings on the right with one leading into the loading bay in the station.

Brunel University/Mowat, Clinker, Wookey Locomotive Collection,

rail. In 1956 Chinnor Cement Co still had daily coal deliveries. Lime production ceased in 1974.

The line became part of the London Midland Region in 1979 when it had some 76,000 tons of minerals passing along it.

The cement works were founded by one William Elijah Benton, a mining engineer from Acton, in 1908. It began as a lime burning business that in 1919 became also a manufacturery for cement. The chalk was quarried at a rate of 400,000 tonnes a years to make 225,000 tonnes of cement. The works is now a subsidiary of the giant Rugby Portland Cement Company. As the trains of coal and gypsum arrive at the works they are pushed onto the firm's private siding where they run by gravitation to a wagon tippler. After emptying, the wagons roll onwards to the empties' sidings at the west end of the works where a BR loco drew them out.

Before the GCR line was lifted in 1966 the minerals came via Woodford Halse and Banbury. After then they had to travel south to Willesden Yard, then over to Acton (WR) Yard from where they departed as a loose coupled train of thirty to forty wagons sometimes including gypsum. They ran at 7.40 am on Mondays to Fridays behind a class 31 from Old Oak Common. The branch was run as a long siding with a key to unlock the sidings ground frames. The most awkward was Wainhill Crossing which is approached on a 1 in 73 gradient but also has a speed restriction of 5 mph and a requirement for the train to stop as a crew member opens and closes the gates.

Chinnor in June, 1957, some rails of the loading bay line are just visible in the grass in the forground.

R M Casserley

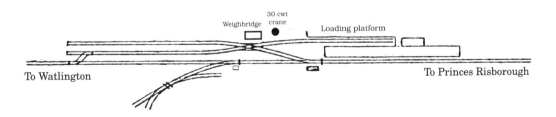

The simple track layout at Chinnor with the siding leading off to the cement works

Hymek class 35 no 7029 at Chinnor cement works after bringing in the daily coal and gypsum (ex-Kegworth, Nottinghamshire). The lorry is a Foden of Rugby Cement Co. The photograph was taken on October 10, 1973.

Geoff Gamble

A variety of diesel power on the branch, with North British loco type 2 (class 22) no D6355 leaving Chinnor propelling a brake van back to Princes Risborough. Note Chinnor to Bledlow Ridge road bridge in the process of re-decking and widening, being closed to traffic on April 11, 1968.

Geoff Gamble

In bright winter sunlight of December 28, 1978 diesel 31136 runs round at Chinnor pushing the wagons back and passing the smoke emanating from the Guard's stove, probably burning the bacon!

Geoff Gamble

Official opening train under C&PRR operation, hauled by 08011 'Haversham' as it prepares to leave Chinnor.

G Gamble

Pannier tank '5700' class no 5766 on the Watlington branch in the late Fifties.

Peter Waylett

Kingston Crossing Halt facing the Chinnor direction on June 12, 1957. All of the Halts were built 70ft in length.

R M Casserley

The station design was virtually replicated along the line, this view at Aston Rowant looking in the Princes Risborough direction. Note the pointsman's shelter on the right facing the points for entrance to the goods yard.

R C Riley

Aston Rowant

Situated just over six miles down the branch alongside the main road from Oxford to High Wycombe. It had a goods yard on the 'up' side with two sidings. It was remotely situated from the village of its name and after closure was more isolated still in an increasingly road concentrated age. It was therefore shortly after closure demolished and the ground used as a dump for road materials.

The roar of the nearby M40 emphasises still further how far from the idyll portrayed in these pages the site has now become.

PRINCES RISBORO' and WATLINGTON (One class only).—Great Western.															
Miles	**Down.**		**Week Days.**						Miles	**Up.**		**Week Days.**			
	Paddington Station,	mrn	mrn	mrn	aft	aft	aft	mrn			mrn	mrn	mrn	aft	aft	aft
—	41a London ....dep.	6d55	8 10	1145	2 40	4 26	24	.9 0	—	Watlington ¶........dep.	7d38	8 55	1140	2 55	4 39	6 55
—	Princes Risboro' ¶ ...dep.	8d18	9 42	1258	4 0	5 19	7 32	1025	2¾	Aston Rowant	7d46	9 3	1148	3 3	4 47	7 3
3¾	Chinnor....................	8d28	9 52	1 8	4 10	5 29	7 42	1035	5¼	Chinnor.............[636	7d53	9 10	1155	3 10	4 54	7 10
6¼	Aston Rowant............	8d35	9 59	1 15	4 17	5 36	7 49	1042	9	Princes Risboro' ¶41a.arr.	8 d 3	9 20	12 5	3 20	5 4	7 20
9	Watlington ¶........arr.	8d43	10 7	1 23	4 25	5 44	7 57	1050	43¾	41a London (Paddington) ar	9d15	1035	1 20	4 30	6 27	9 30

¶ "Halts" at Bledlow Bridge, between Princes Risboro' and Chinnor; Kingston Crossing, between Chinnor and Aston Rowant; and Lewknor Bridge, between Aston Rowant and Watlington.   d Mondays only.

Branch timetable in 1904 Bradshaw

Bill Simpson Collection

Aston Rowant with all the charm of the country station in summer. This view taken on June 12, 1957.

R M Casserley

Pannier tank no 5766 calls with an afternoon train from Princes Risborough, its single coach train received without anticipation by the deserted station.

R M Casserley

Lewknor Bridge Halt the last call before Watlington seen here on October 14, 1957 looking in the Princes Risborough direction.

R M Casserley

Arriving from Princes Risborough is the Watlington goods behind ex-Great Eastern Railway J15 no 65390. This engine was from Neasden shed before its scrapping and worked the branch during the summer of 1957.

R M Casserley

Watlington station on June 29, 1957 with the cattle dock and end loading platform in the foreground
R M Casserley

Pannier tank no 5715 runs round its train at Watlington on June 21, 1952. Note the carriage shed on the right.

R C Riley

Watlington on September 23, 1951 with a view of the timber goods shed. As the line had been designated to work on the one engine in steam principle there is a notable absence of signals on the branch. Although it did later utilise electric train staff working. Apparently lifeless, a pannier tank engine is stored behind the wagon on the siding of the locomotive shed.

R C Riley

Watlington

Somewhat distant from the small market town of Watlington, providing good business for carrier carts; the station at Watlington was an elementary rustic affair with one short platform and the same station building pattern as Aston Rowant and Chinnor.

The station enjoyed the prominence of a 'slip' coach before the Second World War from the 7.10 Paddington - Birmingham, train.

The branch locomotive was held together with the auto coach in a corrugated iron shed with partly open sides. To supply water, a water tank wagon was kept in the station yard and the GWR later installed one of their standard water columns. The loco shed building, that was timber, was destroyed by fire in 1906. Loco allocation at Watlington ended in June 1957.

The goods yard had three sidings and all points were worked from a ground frame. On approach there was one fixed distant signal, similar to the Abingdon branch. Signalling was controlled by a ground frame to operate the points in the station yard.

The sadness of last day working as pannier tank no 4650 takes the 7.15 train from Watlington to Princes Risborough on June 29, 1957.

R M Casserley

Engine no 4638 pulls into Watlington on July 19, 1952.

H C Casserley

Watlington June 12, 1957, a haze of smoke from the unseen engine drifts over the roof of the decaying station, there in an air of resigned melancholy.

R M Casserley

Ground plan of Watlington station in 1922. Some distance from the town but ideal for nearby Shirburn Castle. Locomotive shed building was on the same siding directly opposite the carriage shed.

Reproduced by kind permission of Ordnance Survey Crown Copyright NC/01/479

S.P

Tk.

W.M.

Goods Shed

S.B.

45
·644

Watlington
Station

ter Box

46
1·085

47
·844

Ex-GWR pannier no 5766 arrives at Watlingon on June 12, 1957 with the 2.15 ex Princes Risborough.

R M Casserl

Days of the Great Western Railway when 2055 brought the 10.14 am train from Princes Risborough on June 17, 1939. No doubt the baskets contain some local harvested produce.

H C Casserley

Wallingford station on June 7, 1933 with Armstrong '517' no 1469 class waiting with a train for Cholsey. The engine received a Belpaire firebox in June 1931 but was withdrawn in September 1933. Its final years seem therefore to be working the Wallingford branch.The same class also worked the Watlington branch

Phil Rogers Collection

CHAPTER 6

WALLINGFORD

This was the first narrow gauge branch from the original GWR main line between London and Bristol. The station on the main line from which the Wallingford branch was to be built was opened in June 1840, first of all as Wallingford Road. It was later rebuilt three quarters of a mile further west and named simply Moulsford, opening on July 2, 1866. This was then the junction station for the Wallingford & Watlington Railway of July 25, 1864 of 3 miles 20 chains. As the name suggests, the intention on the survey was to carry the branch to Watlington, nine miles. It was absorbed by the GWR in 1872.

A Mr Thomas White won the contract to build the line for £20,232 to what was planned then as a temporary terminus at Wallingford.

The line ran with a square train staff and one-engine-in-steam system.

When the main line was quadrupled to Didcot the Moulsford station was replaced with the present station at Cholsey and the branch was consequently shortened by three-quarters of a mile. The Wallingford trains used a bay at the west end and ran through attractive but unremarkable countryside.

Amongst special traffic on the branch were trains of milk tanks from the CWS Creamery.

The branch closed to passengers on June 15, 1959.

In connection withWallingford Carnival

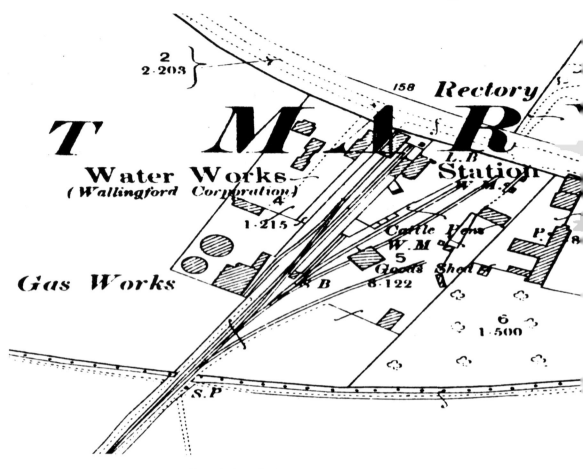

Ground plan of Wallingford station in 1898.
Reproduced by kind permission of Ordnance Survey Crown Copyright NC/10/479

June 17, 1967 the branch line service to Wallingford was restored for the day to Cholsey & Moulsford. A half hourly service was operated with a three car dmu set, nos W51406, W59516, W51364.

On Easter Monday of the following year the GWS ran a steam operated service with the Society's auto train set including no 1466. The train ran twenty journeys and carried nearly 1,500 passengers.

In 1971 The 2½ mile branch was still in use for a daily freight train nicknamed the 'Wallingford Fly'. The train served the Associated British Maltsters siding about quarter of a mile short of the original terminus. Trains were hauled by class 22 diesel haydraulics, one of these being no 6343. The train originated at Reading at 14.00 reversed at Didcot, propelled Reading traffic into a siding at Cholsey & Moulsford, shunting the yard there, then propelling onto Wallingford, returning to Reading at 16.30.

The engine shed was demolished about 1971. The final operational train on the branch to the ABM Maltings Ltd siding ran on 28 May 1981, when no 31131 propelled its train down the branch and picked up two vans from the factory. On May 31 a six-car dmu formation called the 'Wallingford Wake' performed the rites of last train and the 2½ mile branch ceased to be.

Wallingford station early this century complete with carrier carts and early motor vehicle. Also in the goods yard there appears to be a horse omnibus awaiting business. A fairly long train for the branch is in the station platform headed with the ubiquitous GWR saddle tank.

Phil Rogers Collection

What might have been, a view to the station end that may have been a through station to Watlington and Princes Risborough had local interests suceeded.

Brunel University: Mowat, Clinker, Wookey, Locomotive Collection

The local train approaching the station having just passed under the bridge of the A4130. At its head '1400' class no 1447.

Phil Rogers Collection

Wallingford on March 26, 1959 with a detatched locomotive no 1444

B W L Brooksbank

June 17, 1933 with an interesting assembly of GWR vehicles in the horse dock siding on the right.
Brunel University Mowat, Clinker, Wookey, Locomotive Collection

Wallingford in the Fifties with '1400' class no 1407 in service and a rather splendid gas lamp on the right.

J L Smith Collection

The typical scene of a sunlit moment in the small town station of Wallingford in the 1950's with engine 14XX no 1447 in service.

H C Casserley

The train leaving Wallingford in the early 1950's with 14XX 0-4-2T no 1444.

Laurence Waters

Great Western auto coach for operating lines as seen particularly in south Oxfordshire. This vehicle seen here is preserved at the GWR Society site at Didcot.

Bill Simpson

Junction station for the branch to Wallingford, Cholsey and Moulsford early this century. On the extreme left, near the signalbox, a train can be seen entering the station.

Laurence Waters

Wallingford, the perfectly compact small country station early in the twentieth century, the number on photograp is not the year.

Laurence Waters

The engine bunker, first at Wallingford on June 9, 1959.

R M Casserley

Train crew with 1407 at Wallingford shortly before closure.

R K Blencowe Collection

The final days, overgrown and untidy, a little forlorn the branch train works out the final days of this very attractive little station.

RAS Marketing

	CHOLSEY AND MOULSFORD and WALLINGFORD (1st and 3rd class).—Great Western.																			
Miles.	**Down.**					**Week Days.**													
		mrn	mrn	mrn	mrn	aft	aft	aft	aft	aft	aft	aft	aft	aft	K				
—	Cholsey and Moulsford.....dep.	8 13	8 49	9 23	1038	1237	1 44	3 3	3 43	5 23	6 30	7 28	8 33	9 6	1133	....	....	....	....
2¾	Wallingford.................arr.	8 20	8 55	9 32	1045	1244	1 53	3 10	3 50	5 30	6 37	7 35	8 40	9 13	1140	....	....	....	....
Mls	**Up.**	mrn	mrn	mrn	mrn	non	aft	aft	aft	aft	aft	aft	aft	aft	K				
—	Wallingford................dep.	7 55	8 35	9 2	1015	12 0	1255	2 40	3 23	4 50	6 13	6 57	8 10	8 50	9 50	....	....	....	....
2¾	Cholsey and Moulsford 2,12 arr.	8 2	8 42	9 8	1022	12 7	1 2	2 47	3 30	4 59	6 20	7 6	8 17	8 57	9 57	....	....	....	....
	K Wednesdays and Saturdays.																		

Timetable for Wallingford branch in 1909

Tour de force of the GWR, a 'King William IV' hurtles westwards through Twyford station, junction station for the branch to Henley. The train is passing through the arch built in 1892.

H C Casserley

CHAPTER 7

HENLEY-ON-THAMES

The first possiblity of a railway at Henley came in 1833 with a Tring, Reading and Basingstoke Railway that would have entered Oxfordshire near Watlington and provided a station at the town in its progress to Reading. Nothing however came of this.

The first unsuccessful Bill for a branch from Twyford to Henley was submitted in 1846. In 1847 a second attempt was more fortunate and it received the Royal Assent on July 22, 1847, beset in the middle of a financial crisis for all investement delayed construction of the line until a further Act of August 4, 1853. This enabled work to continue by one A W Ritson throughout the winter 1854-5. The people of Henley managed to raise £15,000 towards the capital for the line.

The railway opened on June 1, 1857 being 4³/₄ miles in length. The terminus was at first called 'Henley', it was changed to Henley-on-Thames from January 1, 1895. To avoid the confusion with Henley in Warwickshire

By the end of 1875 the Faringdon and Henley branches were the last purely broad gauge lines on the GWR east of Bristol.

The work included Shiplake viaduct a 230 yard timber bridge across the Thames, this was converted to cast iron in 1895. This marks the county boundary between Oxon and Berks; Twyford is in Berkshire. There are two stations along the line, one for Wargrave and another for Shiplake two miles from Twyford, Wargrave was added in 1900, 1³/₄ miles from Twyford.

The branch was converted to standard gauge in a single night from 9.30pm to

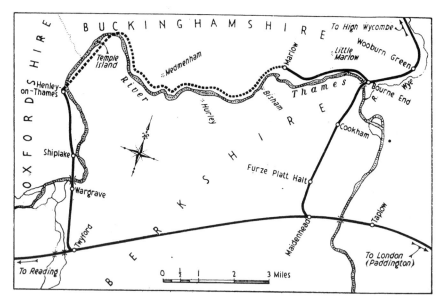

Prospects of connection had the forces opposing not been able to forestall it. The broken line indicates the route the GWR would have built their railway.

Railway Magazine

9.30am on March 24, 1876. On the following day only two early morning passenger trains were suspended.

Between 1896-8 pressure of traffic required an increase to double the track and improvements at Twyford were put in to allow through running from Paddington.

In 1902 there were 19 passenger trains each way on the branch on weekdays with seven each way on Sundays. Locomotive facilities were improved by the installation of a turntable in 1903.

By 1910, in the days before the First World War the branch reached a peak of of twenty-one trains on weekdays and twenty-four on Saturdays and twenty-three on Wednesdays.

In 1904 a 200ft long canopy was added to the 'up' platform and a footpath at the station was deviated and many more sidings were added at Henley.

In 1898 the GWR put forward proposals for a Marlow & Henley Railway to extend the line down the River Thames to join the Marlow - Bourne End branch that was opened in 1873 joining with the Wycombe branch. In the 1890's the GWR viewed with concern the threat of a Metropolitan District

Railway line from Harrow via Beaconsfield to High Wycombe which they opposed.

The proposal did receive popular support from Marlow and Henley townspeople as in effect, the route would be run through on a huge loop with both termini as through stations with improvements in the junction at Twyford. However, owing to the topography the economic route chosen alongside the Thames, a very attractive route, which incensed some interested parties with strong objections. Notably the Leander Rowing Club who considered that commercial interests were despoiling the Thames Valley and works on the line would come close to their clubhouse. This polarised into fierce opposition and became another example of a minority personal interest overruling the popular cause. The GWR did not pursue the idea further during the parliamentary session of 1898, but they did double the branch in expectation of possible success.

The branch was made very popular for the use of those attending the Henley Regatta. This practice began to decline from 1906. The branch was used in that year for pioneering work on Automatic Train Control.

Broad and mixed gauge, Twyford c1875. Additional lines needing a new arch to the bridge were constructed on the right in 1892, see page 153.

Brunel University Mowat, Clinker, Wookey Locomotive Collection

Shiplake station, originally timber was destroyed by fire on August 26, 1891. When the line was doubled in 1898 the station included an island platform. In 1913 the station lamps were converted from oil to gas.

In 1933 Henley had twenty down trains and twenty up trains on weekdays.

During the Second World War ambulance trains ran to Henley with wounded servicemen destined for Kingswood Common. Before and during the war Henley received an evening 'slip' coach from the 7.40 from Paddington becoming the 8.9 from Taplow.

Steam haulage was displaced from the branch on October 6, 1958 when the first diesel workings began.

The line was returned to a single track once more on June 16, 1961. Henley station closed to goods on September 7, 1964. Shiplake and Wargrave stations became partly unstaffed from January 31, 1965.

A new signalling installation, believed at that time to be the first in the world with electronic interlocking equipment was brought into use on the five mile Henley branch for trials in 1962.

Working from an illuminated control panel in the signalbox the signalman would set his route by first turning the entrance switch and then pressing the exit button for the route required. If the route is free to be set up, the relevant point levers become unlocked, permitting the signalman to set the points to the appropriate positions. Once the points are properly set, bolted and detected, they become electronically locked and provided all the other safety conditions are fufilled the signals concerned then clear automatically. Route locking becomes progressively effective once a route has been called and the points in it become set and locked.

From March 20, 1972 signalling was controlled from Reading Panel Box.

New development at the Station at Henley between Hallmark Cards Limited and British Rail Property Board provided a new station with a 200 space car park. This provided Hallmark with a new UK and European Headquarters. The company took over the space where once the locomotive facilities stood with the engine turntable.

The line still prospers with some twelve trains daily and continues as the last surviving network branch line in Oxfordshire.

Shiplake intermediate station on July 7, 1958.

H C Casserley

Shiplake station in 1962 looking towards Henley.

A Smith

Shiplake station in 1962 looking towards Twyford.

A Smith

Henley terminus in the Fifties with former GWR AEC railcar in attendance inside the station building.

Laurence Waters

TWYFORD and HENLEY-ON-THAMES—(Third class only)

The Henley branch as portrayed in Bradshaw's Guide in its heyday before the First World War in 1904.

Bill Simpson Collection

The Henley branch on September 8, 1954 with the 12.52 to Twyford hauled by pannier no 5772.

R M Casserley

On July 29, 1956 the 5.44 from Twyford to Henley nears Ruscombe behind ex-GWR pannier 0-6-0T no 3723.

P Waylett

Vintage GWR with cabless 'Metro' tank leaving with a fine array of coaches with footboards early this century.

John Crocker

Much of what Henley was about and much rebuilding was done at the station to accommodate Regatta days. A scene from the genteel world of 1910, a world that would change drastically for ever a few years later, 'never such innocence again' as observed by poet Philip Larkin. The hipped roof building near the trees is on railway land, close by the turntable.

Close-up view of the station building, the former elegence of the station reduced somewhat with concrete lamp posts.

A Smith

Terminus end at Henley in 1964, what a splendind array of period posters whilst the clock is held at the time of 1.40 pm.

A Smith

Defunct locomotive shed in 1964 used to store vans.

A Smith

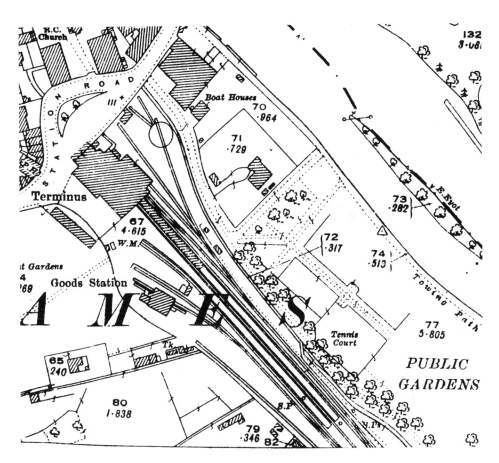

Ground plan of Henley in 1925, the area of loco shed and turntable was taken over by Hallmark Cards.

Reproduced by kind permission of Ordnance Survey Crown Copyright NC/01/479

HENLEY BRANCH.

STATIONS.				WEEK DAYS.								SUNDAYS.					
TRAINS LEAVE	a.m.	a.m.	a.m.	p.m.		p.m.	p.m.	p.m.	p.m.		a.m.		p.m.		p.m.	p.m.
HENLEY	7 15	8 35	10 45	12 40	..	3 40	4 40	5 5	5	..	8 0	..	1 45	..	5 20	7 40
Shiplake	7 21	8 40	10 50	12 45	..	3 45	4 55	6 10	6 10	..	8 14	..	1 58	..	5 35	7 45
Twyford .... Arr.	7 30	8 47	10 58	12 53	..	3 55	5 5	6 20	6 18	..	8 14	..	1 58	..	5 35	7 55

STATIONS.				WEEK DAYS.							SUNDAYS.				
TRAINS LEAVE	a.m.	a.m.	a.m.	p.m.	p.m.	p.m.	p.m.	p.m.	p.m.		a.m.		p.m.	p.m.	p.m.
Twyford	8 5	8 55	11 15	2 2	4 25	5 15	6 30	8 25		..	10 55	..	3 25	6 0	8 25
Shiplake		9 5	11 20	2 10	4 33	5 23	6 38	8 35		..	11 3	..	3 33	8 8	8 35
HENLEY Arr.	8 15	9 10	11 30	2 15	4 40	5 30	6 45	8 40		..	11 10	..	3 40	6 15	8 40

Henley branch timetable in 1862

Henley in the summer of 2001 with 166 turbo operating the branch. To the left the superb Imperial Hotel looks down resolutely.

Bill Simpson

The Henley of the present day, neat but without the elegence of former days

Bill Simpson

Wargrave a fine small station diminished to unmanned Halt status, but at least the village retains a good train service

Bill Simpson

Twyford in 2001, a strong robust building style of the confident GWR of the early twentieth century.

Bill Simpson

The Faringdon branch about 1910. The branch line engine is apparently dealing with matters in the goods yard whilst its train awaits its return in the platform.

Laurence Waters Collection

The junction station for Faringdon was Uffington, this view on May 4, 1957 looking towards Swindon. The Faringdon branch can be seen curving away on the right

R M Casserley

CHAPTER 8

FARINGDON BRANCH

Faringdon Road station 63½ miles from London and, for five months, the terminus of the London division of the construction of the GWR.

The town seriously lost out on the arrival of the railway as it had gained economically from being on a busy coaching route to the west. The coaching routes of the entire country were seriously affected by railway competition. So that towns that had not directly received a railway became isolated by the affect of this.

Faringdon had hoped for a branch from the proposed extension of the Witney Railway to Cheltenham in 1861. This was opposed by the GWR who forced the scheme to end in a truncated form at Fairford.

A local company was eventually successful and the Faringdon branch opened from Uffington, which was a new station newly sited from Faringdon Road, to the town of Faringdon on June 1, 1864 in broad gauge. The railway was 3 miles 49 chains long without any intermediate station. It was the property of the Faringdon Railway Co until 1886

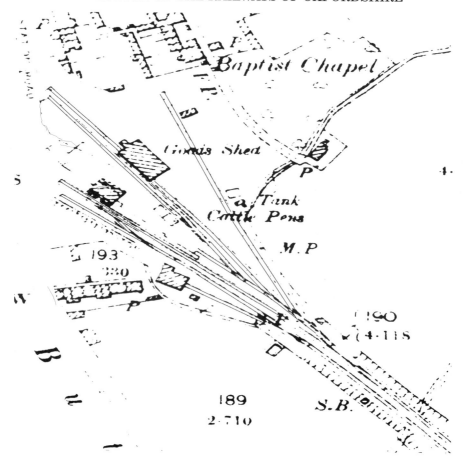

Ground plan of the branch terminus in 1899.
Reproduced by kind permission of Ordnance Survey Crown Copyright NC/01/479

when it was absorbed by the GWR. By that time it was the last section of broad gauge east of Bristol and was converted on August 10, 1878. Local contractor for building this line was Malachi Bartlett.

The line closed to passenger traffic December 31, 1951 which had been running at six trains each way daily.

Freight traffic ceased on July 1, 1963 and the track was removed the following year.

Detail from photograph on page 166.
Laurence Waters Collection

View from the terminus end at Faringdon on April 26, 1959 when a special train ran for the Railway Enthusiasts Club. The engine used was ex-GWR saddle tank no 1365. The branch closed to passengers in 1951.

H C Casserley

The locomotive detatched from its train.

H C Casserley

A view at Faringdon similar to the one of 1910 taken in 1933.
Brunel University/Mowat Clinker, Wookey Locomotive Collection

Uffington looking in the Didcot direction on May 4, 1957.

R M Casserley

Deserted platforms at Faringdon on April 15, 1958. The station building was a remarkably simple design and uniquely effective. It was designed and built by Malachi Bartlett in the Oxfordshire limestone from Witney.

H C Casserley

Local train arriving at nearby Challow station on July 3, 1958 behind 6826 4-6-0 'Nannerth Grange'.

Laurence Waters

Challow, looking towards Didcot May 4, 1957. A station rebuilt in 1934 to accommodate platform loops from the main line.

R M Casserley

The saddle tank special prepares to leave Faringdon on its return to Uffington.

H C Casserley

Arriving back at Uffington with the small water tanks needing replenishing

H C Casserley

UFFINGTON and FARINGDON (1st and 3rd class).—Great Western.

Miles	Down.		mrn	mrn	B	mrn	mrn	aft	aft	aft	aft	aft	aft	aft	aft				NOTES.
																			Week Days.
—	Uffington ......dep.		7 45	8 45	9 45	1018	1133	1225	1 50	2 41	3 59	6 29	7 18	8 6	9 15	....	....	....	
3¼	Faringdon .....arr.		7 55	8 52	9 52	1025	1140	1232	1 57	2 48	4 9	6 36	7 25	8 13	9 22	....	....	....	
Mls	**Up.**		mrn	mrn	mrn	mrn	non	aft	aft	aft	aft	aft	aft						B Runs on the first
—	Faringdon .....dep.		6 45	8 12	9 22	11 8	12 0	1 27	2 20	3 23	5 55	7 40	8 55	....	....	....	....		Tuesday of each month.
3¼	Uffington 2, 12 arr.		6 53	8 20	9 30	1116	12 8	1 35	2 28	3 31	6 3	7 47	9 3	....	....	....	....		

Timetable of Faringdon trains in 1909.

Bill Simpson Collection

The area much contested over through the years for a direct line to Cheltenham. The Witney Railway had hoped for support from the GWR for a through line with a branch to Faringdon. All was to no avail, the GWR never saw any advantage in such a line, but fought attempts by the LNWR (heavy lines) to force such a line through.

Bill Simpson Collection

View from Platform of Faringdon Good shed

R M Casserley

A train on the Wantage Tramway hauled by Manning Wardle 0-4-0ST no 7 approaching Wantage on June 17, 1939. Note the striped road lamp.

H C Casserley

Engine no 5, 'Shannon' of the Sandy & Potton Tramway, with extended chimney, May 10, 1930.

H C Casserely

CHAPTER 9

WANTAGE TRAMWAY

The Wantage Tramway Company was incorporated on November 10, 1873. Being the first to take advantage of the new Tramways Act of 1870. The main line station of Wantage Road was some 2³/₄ miles away and the intention was to build a tramway from Wantage to this station.

It was built and opened to goods traffic on October 1, 1875 and to passengers on October 10 of the same year in standard gauge.

It was originally designated for horse drawn vehicles but mechanical traction was authorised on June 27, 1876. On August 1, 1876 a steam tram was introduced for passenger traffic which made the Wantage Tramway the first in Britain to adopt mechanical traction. The former Sandy & Potton Railway loco 'Shannon' was purchased from the LNWR on May 15, 1878 for £365 and became no 5 of the WT.

The wheels and motion were enclosed by sheeting in accordance with tramway regulations. New cylinders were fitted in 1882 and the loco underwent major repairs at Swindon in 1896.

By the turn of the century the line was carrying about 38,000 passengers annually. It was however with the introduction of GWR road omnibuses that brought its end for that purpose on July 31, 1925. Nevertheless it con-

At Wantage Road station on June 17, 1939. Engine no 7 0-4-0 ST Manning Wardle of 1888, it formerly worked on the construction of the Manchester Ship Canal. At the closure of the Wantage Tramway it was purchased by A R Adams & Son of Newport in Monmouthshire.

H C Casserley

tinued to be used for goods traffic. It survived through the depressed Thirties until December 21, 1945 when it was closed. It had usefully carried coal for the Wantage gasworks and petrol.

Early in 1945 the only locomotive still in use was no 7 making four return journeys on weekdays and some on Saturdays. Engine no 5 was still in shed at Wantage. This engine received substantial damage in 1938.

On April 25, 1946 the Company's plant and equipment was sold. The line was dismantled in 1946.

The engine 'Shannon' was purchased by the GWR for £100 who placed it in statuesque immobility on Wantage Road station.

The Wantage Tramway Company was dissolved on July 18, 1947.

'Shannon' was repainted in 1961 by the Western Region of British Railways in a liv-ery of apple green for the boiler and cab. The wheels and frame were finished in black and the coupling rods and eccentric rods in vermillion. On the side of the cab 'WT Co No 5' appeared in gold leaf. The buffer beams were painted in a darker shade of red and the buffers and copper cap to the chimney were highly polished. It remained on the station until December 31, 1965 when it passed over to the Great Western Railway Society at Didcot where it remains. It took part in the Stockton & Darlington 150th year Railway Celebration Parade at Shildon under its own steam, in August 1975. On that day it passed through the crowds as the oldest locomotive under its own power.

After being rebuilt with four tracks in the 1940's Wantage Road station was finally closed on December 7, 1964

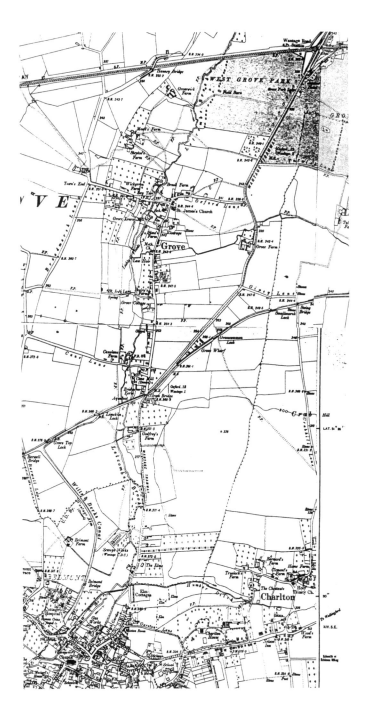

The route of the Wantage Tramway in 1922.
Reproduced by kind permission of Ordnance Survey Crown Copyright NC/01/479

Locomtive no 7 outside the shed, and sundry wagons at the Wantage terminus on June 17, 1939

H C Casserley

Locomotive no 7 by Manning Wardle, May 10, 1930

H C Casserley

A crossing by the junction of the goods branch as no 7 drifts by on May 17, 1939.

H C Casserley

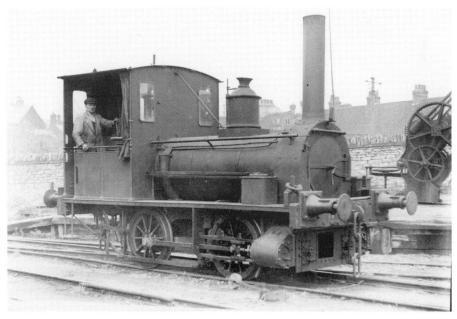

A locomotive that proved to be a hardy survivor. Built by George England in 1857 for the Sandy & Potton Tramway and called 'Shannon'. Bought by the LNWR no 1104 (1863 duplicate list) once worked on the Cromford and High Peak Railway in 1863. Then went to work in Crewe Works from whence the WTR purchased in in 1878 calling it 'Jane'. At the present day it is held at the GWR Society site at Didcot.

H C Casserley

Clearly the tramway role as an assemblage headed by no 7, moves along the road to Wantage
alongside road vehicles on June 17, 1939.

H C Casserley

As above, having passed by the photographer.

H C Casserley

A lone no 7 near Wantage on June 17, 1939, note the lightly spiked tramway track .

H C Casserley

Dreaming of the days of people and conversations, as they sat exchanging the views profound and trivial, within the confines of these elegent little carriages hauled sedately by the 2-2-0 OC Matthews Patent Steam Tram along otherwise silent roads. This view of sad decline was taken on May 10, 1930, before all was broken up by W C Keen & Co, Bristol, probably the year after this photograph.

H C Casserley

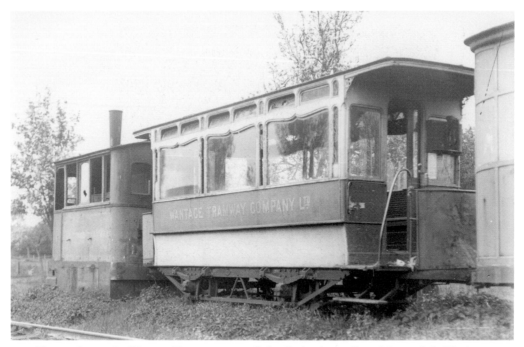

The coaches on the Wantage Tramway carry all the distinctive styling of the coach builder's art in miniature. Ornate window frames and art nouveau stained glass toplights. It is hard to imagine a more enchanting sight as they moved along the road in reflecting glow of flickering oil lamps in a summer twilight.

H C Casserley

In stately isolation after a hard working life 'Shannon' watches other trains go by on Wantage Road station on September 6. 1952.

H C Casserley

Steam Locomotive Scrapyard 1974

Motionless in obedient rows
they stand in unscheduled time
with puzzled expressions gazing through inglorious grime
as they await the cutter's torch.
A sense of movement remains
to mock the rust hard wheels
that once sped through shimmering threads of rail
bringing daily papers, burden of long goods trains, the morning
mail, journeys home, departure to the seaside, summer weekends;
to reach the cindery stillness of this yard
where sunlight flakes the dry entrances of their dark interiors,
the labyrinths of steam.
Do they dream inside this hunk of mechanisation?
Does that fixed expression still see the distances arriving?
Between high girders or approaching a mountain chain,
drifting beneath vaulted arch stations or on a quiet siding.
They have made the last homeward run
the last glow has embered
the last defiant expression done.
And what is left is all of what we knew
of occasions from that shared time
uniquely personal, that they passed through,
now reached its terminal decline.

Bill Simpson

Bibliography

A History of the Railways of Oxfordshire vol 1 (The North) ,
Bill Simpson (1997). Lamplight Publications
History of the Great Western Railway, E T MacDermot, MA (1927)
 Ian Allen
Princes Risborough - Thame - Oxford Railway, Richard Lingard (1978) Oxford
Publishing Co
The Railway Heritage of Britain, Gordon Biddle and O S Nock (1983)
Sheldrake Press Limited
Oxfordshire Past and Present, Laurence Waters & Tony Doyle (1992) Past &
Present Publishing Ltd
Railway Magazine

Addendum

Corrections to volume 1

P35 Train is going south, north of Banbury, signalbox Banbury
North.

P160 The train is on the avoiding line at Kingham heading for
Chipping Norton and Banbury. Note Kingham station left in the
distance.

P162 Handborough for Blenheim station, the view is looking
towards Yarnton

Index

Lamplight Railway Histories

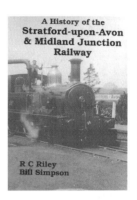

A History of the
Stratford-upon-Avon
& Midland Junction
Railway

R C Riley
Bill Simpson

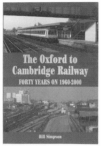

The Oxford to
Cambridge Railway
FORTY YEARS ON 1960-2000

Bill Simpson

The Oxford to Cambridge Railway
Forty Years On 1960 - 2000

Following on from Bill Simpson's Oxford Cambridge Railway histories in the eighties to look how the line has changed to the present day. With some reflections of the days of steam. All held in 144 pages on gloss art inside full colour laminate cover.
£12.95 plus p&p £2.00

A History of the Stratford-upon-Avon and Midland Junction Railway

Compiled by Dick Riley and written by Bill Simpson, This superb volume of a cross country route from Broom Junction to Olney is contained in 160 pages. Beautifully bound in gloss art paper with over two hundred photographs, line illustrations, maps, etc, many never seen before. A must for anyone interested in the railways in Northamptonshire, Warwickshire and Oxfordshire.
£24.95 plus p&p £2.50

A History of the
Railways of
OXFORDSHIRE
Part 1: The North
Bill Simpson

A History of the Railways of Oxfordshire
Part 1: The North

First of a two volume history of Oxfordshire railways complete with over 250 photographs, maps, diagrams and text. Included are the ironstone works railways and the Bicester Military Railway related in 192 pages.   **£19.95 plus p&p £2.50**

The Wolverton to Newport Pagnell Branch

A fascinating branch line history with over a hundred photographs, maps, diagrams, timetables and an additional section on the Wolverton & Stony Stratford Tramway. An intensely packed little book of 144 pages tells the story of this four mile branch that so closely served the Wolverton works employees and their families for many years.   **£8.95 plus p&p £1.25**

The Wolverton to
Newport Pagnell Branch
by
Bill Simpson

The Dunstable Branch

Branch line of the LNWR that was later extended to Luton by the Great Northern Railway. The story of this seven mile branch told with over a hundred photographs, maps, timetables, digrams in 143 pages. Also covering the narrow gauge sand quarry railway which is now the preserved Leighton Buzzard Narrow Gauge Railway   **£8.95 plus p&p £1.25**

The
Dunstable Branch
Leighton Buzzard - Dunstable - Luton
by Bill Simpson

The Banbury to Verney Junction Branch

Re-printed several times this popular history of the twenty-one mile branch from Verney Junction to Banbury includes the stations of Buckingham and Brackley in a hundred photographs, with maps, timetables and plans in 176 pages. A feature of the line being that diesel trains were introduced in 1956!   **£8.95 plus p&p £1.25**

The Banbury to Verney Junction Branch
by Bill Simpson

Available from

Lamplight Publications

260 Colwell Drive, Witney, Oxfordshire. OX8 7LW

'I could write a book about it!'

How often have you thought about that? With Lamplight Publishing Services this is achievable.

You may have been tracing your family history and if you having reached a satisfying conclusion surely the results deserve to be published? It will then be available to succeeding generations of your family for many years to come, a valuable source of reference with special areas included for new dates in your family's history.

Possibly you may have an absorbing lifelong hobby in which you have carried out a great deal of research that you would like to see published in a referrable form. Or perhaps a volume of poems with illustrations. Lamplight Publishing Services can produce any type of printed books from booklets to hardback in black and white or full colour

All work will be undertaken by us with regular consultations with you, you supply the raw material and we will supply an estimate for work to a finished product delivered to you for distribution. Work will be produced by people with a lifetimes experience that will ensure a professionally produced book.

For details write to the address below giving some indication of what you have in mind.

Lamplight Publishing Services
260 Colwell Drive
Witney
Oxfordshire
OX8 7LW